W9-CNA-639

J960
MUR

BAKER & TAYLOR

# AFRICA

## DR. JOCELYN MURRAY

UPDATED BY BRIAN A. STEWART

### THIRD EDITION

CHELSEA HOUSE
PUBLISHERS
An imprint of Infobase Publishing

*Cultural Atlas for Young People*
AFRICA
*Third Edition*

**Copyright © 2007 The Brown Reference Group plc**

**Chelsea House**
An imprint of Infobase Publishing
132 West 31st Street
New York, NY 10001

**Library of Congress Cataloging-in-Publication Data**
**available upon request.**

ISBN: 0-8160-6826-7

ISBN 13 digit: 978-0-8160-6826-5

Set ISBN: 978-0-8160-7218-7

**The Brown Reference Group**
(incorporating Andromeda Oxford Limited)
8 Chapel Place, Rivington Street
London EC2A 3DQ
www.brownreference.com

**For The Brown Reference Group plc:**
Editorial Director: Lindsey Lowe
Project Editor: Graham Bateman
Editor: Virginia Carter
Design: Steve McCurdy
Senior Managing Editor: Tim Cooke

Printed in Singapore

10 9 8 7 6 5 4 3 2 1

**Artwork and Picture Credits**
Maps drawn by Lovell Johns, Oxford, and Alan Mais, Hornchurch.

Key: t = top, b = bottom, c = center, l = left, r = right

Title page CF. 5 HL/Stephen Pern. 7 Clive Spong. 8 W. Kerremans. 8–9 WF. 10 HL/Patricio Goycolea. 12t SAL/C. Buxton. 12b Biofotos/H. Angel. 14 Dr Graham Speake, Oxford. 14–15 Richard and Adam Hook. 16 Picturepoint, London. 17 WF. 18 Sonia Halliday, Weston Turville, Bucks. 19t Roger Wood, London. 19bl Elsevier Archives. 19br KM. 20bl WF. 20tr CF. 21 Elizabeth Photo Library, London. 22 Spectrum Colour Library, London. 22–23 KM. 24–25 KM. 25b W.H. Brooke/Fotomas Index, London. 26 RHPL/George Rainbird Ltd. 27 KM. 28l Sebastian Münster. 28c,r Hulton Deutsch Collection, London. 29 KM 30tl HL. 30tr Father Kevin Carroll SMA, Cork, Eire. 30bl WF. 30br Aspect Picture Library/Peter Carmichael. 32–33 Chris Forsey. 33t Agence Hoa-Qui, Paris. 34t Zefa Picture Library, London. 34c WF. 34b Aspect Picture Library/Larry Burrows. 35l RHPL. 35b Agence Hoa-Qui, Paris. 36 HL. 36–37 Gallo Images/CORBIS. 37 WF. 38tl Royal Anthropological Institute Photographic Collection, London. 38tc Klaus Paysan, Stuttgart, Germany. 38tr Anne Cloudsley-Thompson, London. 39t (left to right) Pitt Rivers Museum, Oxford; Elizabeth Photo Library, London; Pitt Rivers Museum, Oxford; Elizabeth Photo Library, London. 39b Zefa Picture Library, London. 40t Dr H. Turner, Aberdeen. 40b HL/Sarah Errington. 41 CF. 42t Michael Holford, Loughton, Essex. 42c WF. 42b Dr H. Turner, Aberdeen. 43t WF. 43c Rex Lowden, Stockport, England. 43b Richard and Adam Hook. 44 All photographs by Dr Gerhard Kubik, Vienna. 44–45 WF. 45t,c,b HL. 46–47 KM. 48–49 Chris Forsey. 50 WF. 50–51 RHPL. 53 Sonia Halliday, Weston Turville, Bucks. 54 CF. 54–55 HL. 55 KM. 56 Henri Stierlin, Geneva. 56–57 Chris Forsey. 57 RHPL/John G Ross. 60 WF. 60–61 KM. 62tl Agence Hoa-Qui, Paris. 62tc HL. 62tr WF. 62–63 HL. 63t WF. 63b CF. 64t HL. 64b Magnum/Ian Berry. 65t HL/Sarah Errington. 65b HL. 66tc, bl Museum für Völkerkünde, Vienna. 66–67 Bridgeman Art Library, London. 67l Michael Holford, Loughton, Essex. 67r Museum of Mankind, British Museum, London. 69l HL. 69c,b CF. 70–71 Richard and Adam Hook. 71br CF. 72 HL/A Singer. 74t HL. 74bl WF. 74br Agence Hoa-Qui, Paris. 75tl Roger Wood, London. 75tr RHPL. 75b WF. 76 HL. 78t Aspect Picture Library, London. 78b CF. 79t KM. 79b HL. 80 Syndication International, London. 82–83 KM. 83 Peter Garlake, London. 84t Agence Hoa-Qui, Paris. 84c Syndication International, London. 84b A.A.A. Photo, Paris. 85tl CF. 85tr Zeta Picture Library, London. 85b De Beers Ltd, London. 86 CF. 88t Aspect Picture Library, London. 88b A. Bannister. 89 KM. 90cl AH. 90tr Timothy Beddow/HL. 90br CF.

**List of Abbreviations**
CF = Colorific!, London. HL = Hutchison Library, London. KM = Kevin Maddison. RHPL = Robert Harding Picture Library, London. SAL = Survival Anglia Ltd, London. WF = Werner Forman Archive, London.

# Contents

Introduction 4

Timelines 6

**PART ONE:**
**THE HISTORY OF AFRICA**

Geography of Africa 10

Climate and Vegetation 12

The Earliest Humans 14

The Kingdoms of Africa 16

Greeks and Romans in Africa 18

Europeans in Africa 20

The Portuguese 22

The African Slave Trade 24

The Great Trek 26

Exploration of the Interior 28

Christian Missionaries in Africa 30

Islam in Africa 32

Africa's Religions 34

Distribution of People in Africa 36

African Peoples and Languages 38

Education and Literacy 40

African Art 42

Music and Dance 44

Houses 46

Husuni Kubwa 48

**PART TWO:**
**A REGIONAL GUIDE TO AFRICA**

North Africa 52

Nomadic Life 54

Cairo 56

West Africa 58

A Dogon Village 60

Yoruba Religion 62

Asante Ceremonial Regalia 64

Nigerian Art: Bronze- and Brass-casting 66

W. Central Africa 68

A Mbuti Encampment 70

Northeast Africa 72

Christians in Ethiopia 74

East Africa 76

The Game Parks of East Africa 78

S. E. Central Africa 80

Zimbabwe 82

Mineral Resources 84

Southern Africa 86

Hunter-gatherers 88

Africa in the World 90

Glossary 92

Further Reading/Web Sites 92

Gazetteer 93

Index 95

# Introduction

MOST OF AFRICA MAY ONLY HAVE BEEN KNOWN TO MUCH OF the rest of the Western world for a little more than 100 years. However, the continent has a rich and varied history and culture extending back many centuries before Europeans arrived. Indeed, the earliest human beings, as well as some of the first farmers in the world, seem to have all been Africans. And Arab travelers have visited Africa for nearly 1,000 years.

During the last 1,000 years of African history, a number of great empires and kingdoms have risen, prospered, and fallen. Some of them were in many ways more advanced than the European states of the time. These empires and kingdoms are remembered today in the names of modern African countries such as Mali, Benin, and Zimbabwe.

Climate and geography have significantly shaped African history and culture. Even today, in many regions these factors are a hindrance and barrier to the free movement of people. But they did not prevent Europeans from coming to Africa from the 15th century onward to trade with its states, enslave many millions of its peoples, and explore and colonize its lands.

Like Europe and Asia, Africa has many languages and peoples but, unlike these other continents, African languages were spoken and not written until relatively recently. There were no records of the past written in native languages. How then do we know of Africa's past? Our knowledge has come from four main sources. Firstly, Arab writers and travelers visited the east coast and the lands of West Africa from the 10th century on. Their written accounts, often of daily life as well as of great events, have provided valuable information. Secondly, tracing the movement of languages provides an important clue

when trying to follow developments in the history of ancient Africa. Thirdly, archaeological evidence has been used to piece together African history. The final source of information is the oral (spoken) history of Africans themselves—tales of past events handed down from generation to generation over many centuries.

Art, architecture, and music also help in understanding the cultural history, and in this book you will find articles devoted to these subjects as well as to the history of the African continent.

*Africa* is divided into two main sections. The first, **The History of Africa**, builds up the story of the continent from prehistoric times, through the Ancient Greek and Roman periods followed by Arab and European invasions, to the emergence of all present-day African cultures and societies. Throughout this section there are maps illustrating specific themes or topics in the main text. Many of them are accompanied by charts giving important dates and events in African history.

The second part, **A Regional Guide to Africa**, looks at the countries and peoples of modern Africa. It includes typical atlas-style maps containing details of major towns, cities, rivers, railroads, and country borders. These are accompanied by charts giving key dates in African history since the end of World War II in 1945. Important African towns can be located on these maps using the Gazetteer on page 93.

Our survey of Africa is arranged in double-page spreads. Each spread is a complete story. So you can either read the book from beginning to end, or just dip into it to learn about a specific topic. A Glossary on page 92 explains important historical and African terms used in the book.

**Abbreviations used in this book**

B.C.E. = Before Common Era (also known as B.C.).
C.E. = Common Era (also known as A.D.). c. = *circa* (about).
in = inch; yd = yard; ft = foot; mi = mile.
cm = centimeter; m = meter; km = kilometer.

▶ In Mali, a Dogon villager wears a mask and chestplate covered with cowrie shells as a sign of wealth.

# Timelines

| | Before 10,000 B.C.E. | 10,000–5,000 B.C.E. | 5000–0 B.C.E. | | 200 C.E. | 400 C.E. |
|---|---|---|---|---|---|---|
| **AFRICA'S RULERS AND KINGDOMS** | | | EGYPTIAN CIVILIZATION | | | |
| | | | | GREEK, PHOENICIAN, & ROMAN PERIOD IN N. AFRICA | | |
| | | | | KUSH/MEROITIC EMPIRE | | |
| | | | | AXUM EMPIRE | | |

_Pyramids in Egypt, c.2500 B.C.E._

_Cave drawing from KwaZulu Natal, eastern South Africa, c.500._

| **HISTORY** | "Zinjanthropus" lived in region of Olduvai Gorge (c.2 million B.C.E.). <br><br> Anatomically modern humans in southern and E. Africa (c.200,000–100,000 B.C.E.). | First settlements in Nile Delta (c.8000 B.C.E.). | Great Pyramids built in Egypt (c.2530 B.C.E.). <br><br> Alexander the Great conquers Egypt (332 B.C.E.). | | Axum defeats Meröe (320s). <br><br> Axum becomes Christian kingdom (300–400). | |

_Elongated tin head from Nok culture of northern Nigeria, c.200 B.C.E._

_Church in hole in Axum, c.400._

| **CULTURE AND INDUSTRY** | Earliest stone tools – Ethiopia & E. Africa (c.2.6 million B.C.E.). | Earliest cave drawings yet discovered in Africa, from Apollo 11 Cave, Namibia (c.25,000 B.C.E.). <br><br> Sahara fertile enough for human occupation (c.8000 B.C.E.). <br><br> Egyptian farmers using plows (c.4000 B.C.E.). <br><br> Nok Culture in Nigeria (from 1000 B.C.E.). <br><br> Copper worked south of Sahara (c.500 B.C.E.). <br><br> Ironworking in Kush (c.200 B.C.E.). | | | Axum & E. African coasts trading with Romans & Arabs (100–200). <br><br> Claudius Ptolemy's map of Africa (c.120). <br><br> Beginning of Bantu dispersal in southern Africa (c.100–200). | S.E. Asian crops in E. Africa (e.g., bananas, yams) (c.350). |

6

KANEM & BORNO EMPIRES

PORTUGUESE RULE IN E. AFRICA

BENIN EMPIRE IN W. AFRICA

COLONIAL PERIOD
rule by British, French, Spanish, Portuguese, Belgians, Germans, Italians, Dutch, Turks.

GHANA EMPIRE IN W. SUDAN

MALI EMPIRE IN W. AFRICA

ERA OF TRANSATLANTIC SLAVE TRADE

TAKRUR EMPIRE IN W. AFRICA

SONGHAY EMPIRE

OYO & ASANTE EMPIRES

SHONA EMPIRE & EMPIRE OF MONOMOTAPAS (ZIMBABWE)

MUSLIM RULE IN E., W., & N. AFRICA

The countries of Africa became independent in the 20th century and are now ruled by African leaders.

Great Zimbabwe, a large stone-walled enclosure built by the Shona people c.1200–1400.

Fort Jesus at Mombasa, Kenya, built by the Portuguese 1593–96.

Axum (Ethiopia) threatened by Muslims; isolated from Christian Europe (600–700).

Egypt conquered by Arabs (646).

Carthage conquered by Muslim Arabs (695).

Great Age of Islam in N. Africa begun (800–900).

Muslim "Almoravids" invade Ghana (1087).

Ghana defeated by Sundiata of Mali (1240).

Reign of Mansa Musa in Mali (1307–37); his pilgrimage to Mecca (1324–25).

Portuguese in Kongo (1482).

Bartholomeu Dias rounds Cape of Good Hope (1488).

Portugal established E. Coast forts (from 1509).

Turks occupy Egypt (1517).

Hausa States in Nigeria (Kano/Katsina) (1510–40).

Moroccan invasion of Songhay (1591).

Osei Tutu creates Asante Union (1697).

First contact between Boers & Bantu (1778).

Napoleonic Wars: Battles of the Nile & Alexandria (1798 & 1801).

Fulani Empire in W. Africa (1800–1900).

Congo Free State established by Belgium (1884).

Boer War in S. Africa (1899–1902).

Mau-Mau movement in Kenya (1952–60).

Ghana independent (1957).

French West African Colonies independent (1960).

Portuguese colonies independent (1975).

Zimbabwe independent (1979).

Compound of houses on steep hillsides built by Dogon people in Mali from about 1500.

Trans-Saharan trade expands (from c.800).

Use of iron widespread in Africa (c.650).

E. Africa part of Indian Ocean trade area— visited by Arabs & Chinese (c.800).

Islam established south of Sahara (c.1000).

Slaves exported to N. Africa from Guinea (c.1150).

Early buildings at Great Zimbabwe (c.1200).

Yoruba sculptures at Ife (from 1250).

Ibn Battuta visits Mali (1352).

University at Timbuktu (c.1450).

Asante exports gold north (c.1550–1650).

Portuguese introduce S. American crops (e.g., cassava, maize) to Africa (c.1500).

African porter carrying ivory tusk for Europeans "on safari," c.1850.

British ban on slave trading (1807).

Opening of Suez Canal (1869).

Discovery of diamonds in S. Africa (1874).

First major railway systems built in E. and S. Africa (1880–1900).

# Part One

# The History
of Africa

▲ A carved and polished wooden mask that was used by the Chokwe people of the Democratic Republic of the Congo in religious ceremonies.

▶ Pillars of dried mud in front of the mosque at Jenne in Mali, West Africa. The mosque was built of dried mud on a wooden framework.

# Geography of Africa

AFRICA, THE SECOND LARGEST CONTINENT (after Asia), is more than three times larger than the United States. Its greatest north–south length is 5,000 miles (8,000 km), and its greatest width is 4,650 miles (7,500 km). The equator lies almost across its center, but two-thirds of its area is in the northern hemisphere. Although three-quarters of Africa lies within the tropics, the climate is affected more by altitude, or land height, and distance from the sea (see pages 12–13).

## Formation of the African landmass

Africa once lay at the heart of a supercontinent called Pangea. About 180 million years ago the separate parts of this great continent began to drift apart. The African and Asian parts are divided only by the narrow Red Sea, but the whole of the Atlantic Ocean separates them from the American parts.

The continents are still slowly drifting. In Africa comparatively recent movement has left weak strips, known as fault lines. In eastern Africa, they make up one of the longest "rift systems" in the world (see small map).

At the extreme northwest and southeast of Africa are young mountain ranges. But most of the continent consists of vast flat lands, or plateaus (tablelands), at different levels.

Where the plateaus have many rivers and streams, a large lake sometimes forms at the lowest level, for example, Lake Chad. Around the edges of the plateaus, along the coasts, are narrow plains.

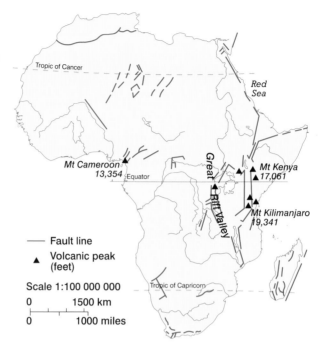

Tropic of Cancer

Red Sea

Mt Cameroon 13,354  Equator

Great Rift Valley

Mt Kenya 17,061

Mt Kilimanjaro 19,341

Tropic of Capricorn

— Fault line
▲ Volcanic peak (feet)

Scale 1:100 000 000

0      1500 km
0      1000 miles

▲ A rift is a steep-sided valley formed as a section of Earth's crust sinks between two or more fault lines. The African rift system runs from the Red Sea into Malawi and Mozambique. Its best-known section is Kenya's Great Rift Valley.

Madeira Islands (PORTUGAL)

Canary Islands (SPAIN)

WESTERN SAHARA (MOROCCO)

**MAURITANIA**
■ Nouakchott

Senegal

Dakar ■ **SENEGAL**
Banjul **GAMBIA** Gambia

Bamak

Bissau ■ Fouta Djallon

**GUINEA-BISSAU**    **GUINEA**

Conakry ■

Freetown ■
**SIERRA LEONE**

Monrovia ■
**LIBERIA**

▶ Africa's coastlines are regular, with few inlets to provide deepwater harbors. Apart from Madagascar, islands are small and few.

For a large continent, Africa has relatively few great rivers, and they often have rapids and waterfalls where they pass over the edges of steep plateaus. Along flatter land, rivers are often winding and have therefore been of little use for long-distance transportation. Like the lakes, they have been useful only for fairly local movement.

◀ Looking down from the Eastern Rift in Kenya. In East Africa there are two main branches of the Great Rift Valley: eastern and western. The Eastern Rift runs past Mounts Kilimanjaro and Kenya, which are extinct volcanoes. In places its walls fall 2,600 ft (800 m) from the plateaus on either side of it.

# Climate and Vegetation

RAINFALL IN AFRICA MAINLY OCCURS IN particular seasons, but it is unpredictable and varies greatly from region to region. Some years there is enough rain for farming, while in others there is none, and droughts occur.

At Africa's extreme north and south the climate is like that in Mediterranean Europe, with distinct seasons. Along the north coast there are wet winters from December to February. In South Africa winter is from June to August.

In the hot deserts of North Africa, northeast Africa, and southwest Africa, there is little rain at any time of the year. The Sahara experiences real extremes of temperature—from more than 90°F (32°C) in July to 0°C (32°F) during the cold season. The tropical rainforests, in West Africa and west central Africa, are always hot and wet, and rain falls most months.

## On plateaus and mountains

Over the rest of the continent, the temperature is largely affected by the altitude of the land and its distance from the sea, rather than by latitude. That is why Africa is much drier and less hot than you might expect. There are some dry, cold periods but no true winters.

North of the equator July is the hottest, driest month. In the south, however, January is hottest. The rains in the northern hemisphere fall around March through April (known as "the long rains") and again in October ("the short rains").

During the rainy season, the rain usually falls very hard. In a typical day there will be heavy rain from nightfall to the early morning, followed by a clear—even sunny—day. (Near the equator night and day are of roughly equal length.) Thunderstorms are frequent, especially in the tropics and around the great lakes (Chad, Victoria, Malawi).

On the plateaus the vegetation varies from forests to grassy plains and drier, rough-grass plains (savanna, or veldt) with acacia and bottle-shaped baobab trees. In the mountain regions bands of bamboo, heather, lichens, and alpine plants occur.

## Changes in vegetation

The vegetation of Africa was once quite different, however. Around 7,000 to 3,000 B.C.E. the Sahara was 15 times wetter than it is today. Many large freshwater lakes formed at this time, sustaining crocodiles, hippos, catfish, and, consequently, hunter-gatherer groups.

◀ South of the dry northern deserts, inland Africa, except for the mountains and rainforests, is dry savanna, with short grasses and thorn trees (acacia). It is perfect country for large animals such as zebras, giraffes, and elephants. Where elephants become too numerous, they can damage the vegetation, as here in Tanzania.

▼ High up on Mount Elgon in western Kenya the vegetation is more alpine than tropical. Plants related to the ragworts of wastelands in temperate regions have evolved these stumpy forms.

▼ ▶ The type of vegetation (right) that grows depends on rainfall (below), temperature (bottom), and type of soil. Where there is little or no rain, plants cannot grow, as in the great deserts of North Africa. In the plateaus and mountains the differences between day and night temperatures are often much greater than between seasons.

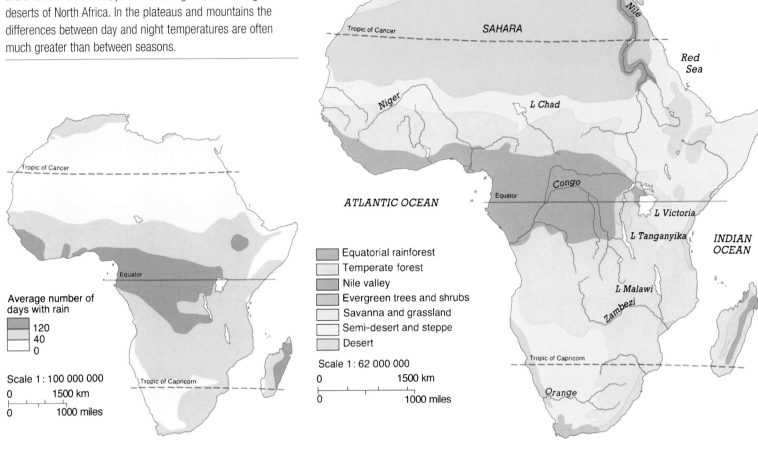

Equatorial rainforest
Temperate forest
Nile valley
Evergreen trees and shrubs
Savanna and grassland
Semi-desert and steppe
Desert

Scale 1 : 62 000 000

0          1500 km
0                1000 miles

Average number of days with rain

120
40
0

Scale 1 : 100 000 000

0          1500 km
0                1000 miles

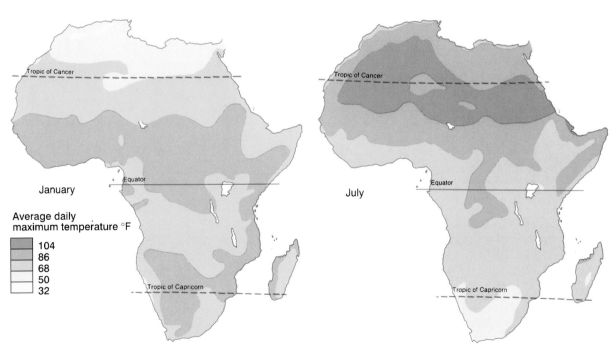

January

Average daily maximum temperature °F

104
86
68
50
32

July

◀ These two temperature maps show that north of the equator it is hotter in July than it is in January, but in the south it is the opposite. Throughout Africa, perhaps more than anywhere else in the world, the vegetation and climate greatly influence the wealth and variety of wildlife and peoples' way of life—affecting whether people are farmers or hunter-gatherers, the type of houses they build, as well as their customs, beliefs, art, and music.

13

# The Earliest Humans

RESEARCH OF PLACES IN EASTERN AND southern Africa where fossils have been found has led us to accept Charles Darwin's claim that Africa must have been the home of the earliest human beings. The most famous site is Olduvai Gorge in northern Tanzania. Fossils from this and other sites tell a story of human development, stretching from 1 million to 5 million years ago.

## Related to monkeys?

It is no longer claimed that humans are descended from monkeys. However, human beings and the apes (gibbons, chimpanzees, gorillas, orangutans) have a common ancestor. Several million years ago a species of apelike creatures developed in two different ways. One group continued to use all four limbs for walking. The other stood erect on two legs, leaving two limbs free for carrying and, eventually, tool-using. We evolved from this second group. A find in Chad in 2001 suggests that the earliest known members of this group lived 7 million years ago.

Skulls of the bipedal (two-footed) apelike hominid *Australopithecus africanus* have been found in eastern and southern Africa. From this stock came *Homo*

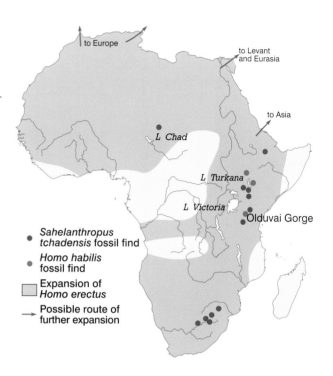

## Sites of the Early and Middle Stone Age

Fossils of *Homo habilis* (known as "handy man"), in association with pebble tools, have been found at sites near Lake Turkana in northern Kenya and at Olduvai Gorge. They have been dated to between 1.8 and 2.5 million years ago. Fossils of *Homo erectus* ("upright man"), with hand axes, have been found widely, and are dated from 250,000 to 1.7 million years ago. The sites marked are those where excavations since 1950 have been made. The Middle Stone Age marks more varied developments in lifestyle over different parts of Africa.

- • *Sahelanthropus tchadensis* fossil find
- • *Homo habilis* fossil find
- ▢ Expansion of *Homo erectus*
- → Possible route of further expansion

*to Europe*
*to Levant and Eurasia*
*to Asia*
L Chad
L Turkana
L Victoria
Olduvai Gorge

▲ Medicine men in trance ritually "control" an eland to harness its religious potency in this scene from a rock-shelter painting in KwaZulu Natal. Rock paintings, found widely throughout Africa, are often linked with earlier hunter-gatherer peoples.

▶ *Homo habilis* men chip at rocks, sharpening them for cutting up game or scraping hides. The game was trapped in a pit or run down by several men. A woman, with her child, gathers berries. Branches were probably collected to make shelters.

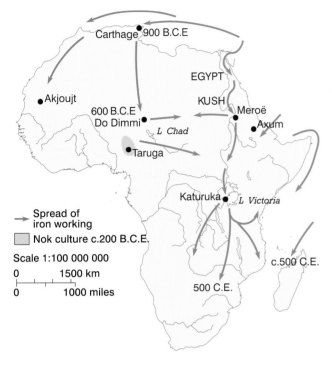

### Bantu culture

Bantu, meaning "the people," is the name given to a group of closely related languages spoken in southern Africa. Archaeological evidence suggests a common culture spread southward between 500 B.C.E. and 1000 C.E., and this is associated with a movement of Bantu speakers from the north.

The culture shares similarities in pottery, agriculture, and the use of ironworking. The Bantu migration may have helped spread ironworking skills into central and southern Africa, starting around 200 B.C.E. By 500 C.E. Bantu culture was common in these areas.

*habilis*, the first toolmaker, from whom *Homo erectus* and *Homo sapiens* are descended.

### The Stone Age and early Iron Age

The remains of many shaped and sharpened pebbles used by *Homo habilis* have been found in Africa. By 1.7 million years ago large almond-shaped stone tools—handaxes—became widespread among *Homo* groups and were probably used for many different tasks. Only about 250,000 years ago (during the Middle Stone Age) did stone tools become more complex. Language was probably developing also, allowing for more effective communication of information (such as the toolmaker's craft). The Middle Stone Age also saw the early development of *Homo sapiens*, whose innovations would allow them to spread to Asia, Australia, Europe, and the Americas.

African hunter-gatherer societies became more sophisticated in the Late Stone Age (which began about 25,000 years ago), when smaller and more exact tools such as bows and arrows were invented.

The Iron Age began in the Middle East around 1200 B.C.E. It spread to the coast of North Africa and then to West Africa along ancient trade routes.

# The Kingdoms of Africa

FROM THE EARLIEST TIMES PEOPLE HAVE lived together to provide for their needs: food, clothing, shelter, and defense. The family—parents and children—is the smallest unit. Several related families together make up a band, clan, or tribe. In some parts of Africa people lived with no more organization than this. The Kikuyu of Kenya and Igbo of Nigeria are successful examples of tribes with village governments in which the "elders" acted as judges or leaders. More usually people joined together in a larger "state" with a strong, central leader such as a chief or king.

## Early kingdoms

Ancient Egypt, which flourished as a civilization as long as 4,500 years ago, was the first of these states. Farther south along the Nile another kingdom, Kush,

emerged around 700 B.C.E. and later grew around the town of Meroë.

Some early kingdoms began when outsiders tried to conquer local clans, who then joined together to defend themselves. In North Africa, when Phoenician traders from the region of present-day Syria founded the city of Carthage, groups of Berbers who were united against them formed in Numidia (now Algeria) and in Mauretania (Morocco).

Later, when Muslim Arabs came to North Africa from the east, kingdoms were founded, both by them and by the local peoples who were defending themselves against the Muslim armies.

Where there was active trading, local leaders organized the collection of taxes and duties. They became rich, gained power, and often made themselves kings. In West Africa, where there

▶ This map shows that there were kingdoms in much of Africa, although not all of them existed at the same time. Almost all were of African origin; only along the northern coastline and in the East African city-states were outsiders the founders. The process of powerful rulers building kingdoms continued right up to the early 19th century, when it was largely stopped by European conquest.

◀ Kings of the early kingdom of Axum on the Red Sea set up tall stones, some more than 100 ft (30 m) high, called monoliths (or stelae) above the royal tombs. Once there were hundreds, but now only about 50 of them remain standing.

By about the first century Axum, controlling Red Sea trade through the port of Adulis, had become a rich and powerful state, from which the inland kingdom of Ethiopia was later to develop. Through the port there were trading connections with Greece, Arabia, and India.

In the fourth century the king of Axum adopted Christianity, but by the seventh century came under the influence of growing Islamic power.

ATLANTIC OCEAN

BUGANDA  Major African kingdom
•  Pre-colonial town

Scale 1 : 62 000 000

0 ————————— 1500 km
0 ————————— 1000 miles

was gold and great markets, traders went across the Sahara as far as Egypt, transporting metals, salt, cloth, ivory, and slaves.

Yoruba and Igbo people, who dyed cloth and made leather and metal goods, formed many small kingdoms. Ghana, and later Mali, Songhay, and Kanem-Borno, were powerful, well-organized kingdoms according to the Muslim travelers and writers who visited them. Islam, the Muslim religion, became well established among the ruling families of all these empires.

## Migration, trade, and city-states

In central Africa, kingdoms were established as the Bantu-speaking peoples began moving east across the region, introducing new crops that were suited to the climate (for example, bananas, yams, and millet). This caused a rapid growth in population in the Congo forests. The kingdoms of Kongo and Ngola were powerful rivals when the Portuguese arrived here in the late 1400s.

Along the coast of East Africa, Arab merchants engaged in a thriving Indian Ocean trade with local African peoples. Many prosperous trading centers, such as Mogadishu and Kilwa, developed to become regional powers. One of the earliest and most powerful was the kingdom of Axum, which controlled parts of southern Arabia.

▼ The entrance to a group of dwellings in Kano city. The walls are made of sun-baked mud. Kano was one of the earliest, and in the 16th century one of the largest, city-states of the Hausa kingdom, Nigeria.

### Major African kingdoms, 3000 B.C.E.–1850 C.E.

**From 3000 B.C.E.** Egypt united under the pharaohs.

**8th century B.C.E.** Phoenicians found Carthage, trading center of their many colonies.

**1st century C.E.** Kingdom of Axum flourishing.

**7th century** Arab conquests along North African coast. Carthage destroyed in 697.

**8th to 9th centuries** Kingdoms of Borno and Kanem flourish to west and east of Lake Chad.

**13th to 15th centuries** Rise of Ethiopia, Kingdom of Mali, Great Zimbabwe.

**From 15th century** Rise of Bantu states in Congo (Democratic Republic of the Congo) and around the East African lakes.

**18th century** Kingdoms of Benin (Nigeria) and also Asante (Ghana) flourishing.

**Early 19th century** Chaka Zulu conquering peoples of southern Africa.

**19th century** Moshoeshoe establishes Lesotho kingdom.

# Greeks and Romans in Africa

THE MEDITERRANEAN IS ALMOST AN inland sea. It has been well traveled for thousands of years. It is not very surprising, therefore, that the peoples who lived on its northern, eastern, and western shores—Romans, Greeks, and Phoenicians—became interested in the lands that lay to the south.

## Egypt under Greece and Rome

The Greeks had traded with Egypt for a long time, and in the fourth century B.C.E. King Alexander the Great of Macedonia (now part of Greece, Macedonia, and Bulgaria) conquered it. In 331 he founded the city named for him. Alexandria, near modern Cairo, became a very great and important center of Greek culture and influence.

After Alexander's death his empire was divided. One of his generals, Ptolemy, made himself king of Egypt, and after him all Egyptian kings were called Ptolemy. Ptolemy I's kingdom was the longest-lasting of the empire.

By the second century B.C.E. the Romans, too, were interested in Egypt, for they were extending their power all around the Mediterranean. In 51 B.C.E. a brother and sister, Ptolemy XIII and the more famous Cleopatra VII, ruled Egypt together, but by 30 B.C.E. the emperor Augustus had made Egypt a Roman province.

## Carthage and Roman Africa

Carthage was founded by Phoenician traders in about 800 B.C.E. near modern Tunis. By the third century B.C.E. the Carthaginians were powerful enough to fight against Roman expansion. In 146 B.C.E., after three long series of battles by land and sea, the Carthaginians were defeated. Rome sacked Carthage and took over the province it called Africa.

The city was rebuilt as a Roman city, but the original people kept their own language and some of their customs. Later Carthage (like Alexandria before) was to become a very important Christian center, in the days before Islam came from Arabia.

▶ The amphitheater at El Djem (south of Carthage) was one of the largest in the Roman Empire. It was built in the third century C.E. to replace an earlier one. As at Rome, gladiators fought and chariots raced to entertain the people.

▼ Long before the Romans came to North Africa, Dougga was a prosperous city. It held a strong defensive position 55 miles (88 km) southwest of Carthage. The Libyan and Punic inhabitants lived alongside the Roman citizens, who built their own amenities, like this temple of the gods Jupiter, Juno, and Minerva.

Cyrenaica, situated 500 miles (800 km) to the west of Alexandria, became a Roman province in 74 B.C.E., together with the island of Crete. It had previously been made a place of Greek settlement by Ptolemy I.

The chief city of Cyrenaica was Cyrene. Farther inland lay another great Roman province, Numidia ("nomads" land), and to the west was Mauritania.

The seminomadic Berbers who lived in the Sahara on the fringes of these two Roman provinces were almost certainly the contacts or go-betweens used by the Phoenicians and Romans to trade with the black peoples living in and to the south of the desert. Rock paintings 2,000 years old that depict horse-drawn vehicles hint at the existence of trade routes between the coast and the interior of Africa.

### The Greek and Roman empires in Africa

**332 B.C.E.** Alexander the Great of Macedonia conquers Egypt. City of Alexandria founded a year later.

**246–241 B.C.E., 221–183 B.C.E.** First and second (Punic) wars between Rome and Carthage.

**218 B.C.E.** Hannibal of Carthage marches across Alps to Italy and defeats Romans in battle.

**146 B.C.E.** Third war between Rome and Carthage. Carthage destroyed. Rome takes over province of Africa.

**74 B.C.E.** Cyrenaica becomes a Roman province.

**47 B.C.E.** Cleopatra VII queen in Egypt.

**44 B.C.E.** Death of Julius Caesar.

**31 B.C.E.** Mark Antony and Cleopatra defeated by Octavian (Emperor Augustus). Egypt now ruled from Rome.

**40 C.E.** Mauretania becomes a Roman province.

▶ Slaves load ivory into the hold of a Roman boat.

▼ There was much trade between North Africa and the Greeks. Later, the Roman Empire depended on Egyptian corn. Other exports were papyrus, flax, olives, dates, wine, and rare animals. This map of 1630 names the parts of Europe, Asia, and Africa that formed the Greek Empire of the second century B.C.E.

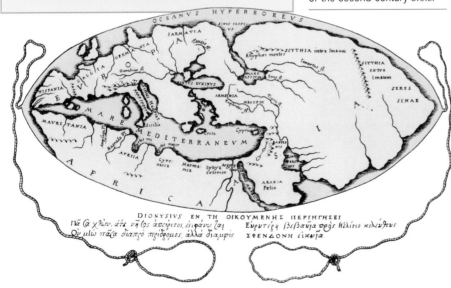

# Europeans in Africa

FOR A VERY LONG TIME, AFRICA WAS AN unknown continent to the people of Europe. Even its shape was like a great question mark. Only the northern coasts, around the south of the Mediterranean, were familiar to Europeans until about 600 years ago.

Claudius Ptolemy, who lived in Alexandria in the second century C.E., published a map of Africa. It was by no means a complete map, but for hundreds of years there was nothing better. The Arabs, who had explored the north and east coasts, knew most about Africa. Ibn Battuta, a Moroccan Berber who lived in the 14th century, wrote of his journeys to Egypt and East and West Africa (as well as to India and China).

## European exploitation begins

In the 15th century, when the Portuguese began looking for a sea route to the East, more information came. The first European to round the Cape of Good

▶ Open-air markets, such as this one in Luxor, Egypt, have for centuries been the great trading places of Africa. Here a tailor works at his sewing machine, producing traditional garments using modern methods.

▼ African artists have often used traditional styles to comment on their new colonial situation. Here, a woodworker from the Democratic Republic of the Congo has carved the Belgian official of the 1920s in his chauffeur-driven car.

## Colonial development from the 1870s

Between 1876 and 1884 there occurred an unofficial scramble among the European nations for regions of Africa that had great mineral resources—gold, diamonds, and copper—and potentially fertile farmland. By 1895 all but the Sahara region had been shared out among seven of them as some 50 separate kingdoms, states, or countries.

1914

European possessions
- Belgian
- British
- French
- German
- Italian
- Portuguese
- Spanish

Hope, the continent's southern tip, was Bartolomeu Dias in 1488. In 1497 Vasco da Gama set sail from Portugal to Calicut, in India, traveling around the coasts of Africa (see page 22). His ship rested in harbors along the way, and here he put up stone crosses, some of which may still be seen today.

Portuguese traders and missionaries soon followed. In West Africa English, French, Dutch, and Swedish traders joined the Portuguese. They exchanged European goods for African products, at first gold and ivory, but by the 18th century the most popular "product" came to be slaves (see pages 24–25). The port-cities at the European end (Liverpool, Bristol, Nantes, Lisbon, Bordeaux, and others) grew wealthy from this barbarous trade.

## Settlers and explorers

In the mid-17th century Dutch farmers were sent to the Cape of Good Hope as employees of the Dutch East India Company to grow food for crews of the Dutch ships that passed on the long journey to Indonesia. After a few years some of the Dutch who wanted to keep cattle moved farther inland from Cape Town. They had, in fact, become settlers.

By 1800 Europeans knew a good deal about the coasts of Africa but they knew very little about the land beyond them. The 19th century was the age of European exploration of the interior, and before the end of the century most of Africa had come under European rule.

The nations that acquired most colonies were Great Britain, France, Portugal, and Germany (until World War I). Spain, Belgium, and the Netherlands also ruled some areas, and later Italy. Liberia (which had strong connections with the United States) and Ethiopia (until it was conquered by Italy in the late 1930s) stayed independent.

## The end of the colonial period

The colonial period lasted only about 80 years. The end of World War II in 1945 saw a decline in the power of Britain, Germany, and France. Nationalism saw a new wave of countries beginning to assert their sense of separate identity. The result was that African colonies began to gain their independence, the first being the Gold Coast (Ghana) in 1957.

Most of the newly independent countries kept a connection with the European country that had once ruled over them, for example, using its language as their own international language, trading with it, and receiving some development aid from it.

Subsequently, the colonial boundaries continually changed with the bargains made between European powers. More than 80 years of colonial rule saw the foundations laid for modern Africa's communications (especially railways), education system, and civil administration. Africans educated and trained by Europeans became the leaders of the independent African nations.

▲ View of Beni Abbes, a small Algerian town. The small dome in the center is the mosque, a visible symbol of Islam. On the hill is the former French fort, recalling the days of colonialism and the French Foreign Legion. Trees and palms shelter and fringe the town.

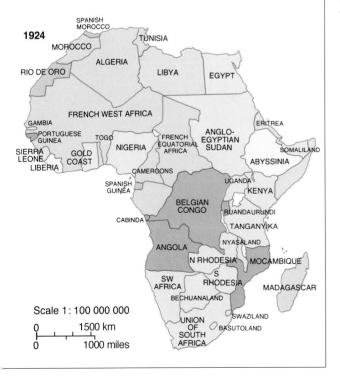

# The Portuguese

THE PORTUGUESE SAILED SOUTH ALONG West Africa from 1415, and Bartolomeu Dias rounded the Cape of Good Hope in 1488. Vasco da Gama took the route to India in 1497, and on his first sea journey called at Mombasa, Malindi, and other East African ports (1498). From the early 15th century until the fall of Fort Jesus at Mombasa in 1698, Portugal was the leading power on the east coast, from Mogadishu in Somalia to Sofala in Mozambique. For nearly 300 years, until 1975, Mozambique remained their trading base.

The Portuguese wanted places where their ships could rest, refit, and take on food and water for the long journey to India. They also wanted profitable trade. The traders lived in coastal settlements where African rulers permitted them to build stores and forts. On the east coast at Mombasa in modern Kenya they built Fort Jesus as a stronghold against the Arabs. In addition, they wanted to provide opportunities for their Catholic missionaries to make converts. In Africa there were pagans, Muslims, and (in Ethiopia) Christians who did not belong to the Roman Catholic Church. Portuguese trade took place both throughout the Indian Ocean and with the African interior (particularly for gold).

## Conquerors and missionaries

The east coast city-states were already part of a trading network controlled by Omani Arabs. Goods came from the Middle East, India, and even from China. To profit from this trade, the Portuguese had to control the cities.

After da Gama's second voyage to India (1502), they began to capture territories by force. In 1505 they occupied Sofala, and in 1506 set up a military base at Kilwa and pillaged Mombasa. These and other cities were taken with much violence and cruelty. But the number of Portuguese officials and soldiers was never more than a few thousand, and there were several revolts against their rule. Muslims were defending not only their religion but also the Arab control of the Indian Ocean network of trade.

Roman Catholic missionaries initially had some success in parts of southern Africa (in Angola-Congo in 1518 an African had been made bishop). But few Africans converted to Christianity in the strongly Islamic cultures of the East African cities. Those who did convert were persecuted by the Muslims.

In 1614 Yusuf, Mombasa's young sultan, was taken to Goa in Portuguese India to receive an education. In 1630 he returned as a Christian with a Portuguese wife, but in 1631 he led a revolt against the Portuguese during which Christians were killed. He died a Muslim in 1637.

One of the most important contributions of the Portuguese in Africa was the introduction of new foods, mainly from Brazil: cassava (manioc) and maize, and fruit and nut trees such as guava, avocado pears, and cashew.

▼ The Portuguese built Fort Jesus from 1592–95 with the help of workmen from India. Even this stronghold did not protect them—after a siege lasting nearly three years, it was taken by the Omani Arabs in 1698.

► On the quayside of an East African port Portuguese and Omani traders haggle over goods unloaded from dhows. The Portuguese needed cloth, beads, porcelain, and metal tools and implements for their trade with African chiefs. Some items they brought from Portugal; other goods were obtained from Omani Arab traders or direct from India.

They traded these goods for gold, which came through Sofala in the south, other metals, ivory, and later slaves (most of whom went to Brazil). They also played a part in local trade up and down the coast, mostly for foods of various kinds and pottery. In the ruins of the old coastal cities plates and coins from China, brought by Arab ships, have been found.

# The African Slave Trade

WHEN EUROPEAN TRADERS FIRST BEGAN buying from Africans, they wanted gold and other metals, and ivory. But they soon found that it was even more profitable to buy and sell African people—that is, slaves.

The new European colonies in the Americas and the West Indies needed workers for the tobacco, cotton, and sugar plantations. African rulers were willing to sell Africans captured from neighboring territories in order to obtain European goods, especially firearms. African states without rifles and ammunition were vulnerable to their neighbors. And so began a terrible trade in human beings.

### Trading in human misery

Slave traders from Spain and Portugal began sending slave ships to West and central Africa in the 16th century. The trade reached its peak in the mid-18th century with Great Britain, France, Portugal, the Netherlands, and Spain heavily involved. Probably more than 12 million men, women, and children were taken from Africa.

Arabs in East Africa also traded in slaves, whom they sold in the Middle East and India, and the Portuguese sold some to Brazil. But the numbers of slaves taken from East Africa were far fewer because at the time that part of the continent was much less heavily populated. In addition to the Africans

captured and forced to embark on the treacherous journey across the Atlantic to the New World, many thousands were killed resisting slaving raids.

### The abolition of the slave trade

The slave trade continued with little check for more than 300 years. But by the early 19th century many Europeans began to oppose it, and laws were passed against trading in slaves—in Great Britain (1807), the United States (1808), and in France and Germany a few years later. It took longer for the use of people as slaves to be abolished, and this happened at different times in different countries. In the United States it occurred only after the Civil War ended in 1865. Slavery was abolished in Cuba (by Spain) and

▼ Of the huge number (more than 11 million) of Africans shipped from Africa as slaves, probably as many as 20 percent died on the journey. They were packed on narrow bunks, often shackled, as here, and unable to move. They were given poor food, ventilation was very bad, and there was no medical care. Even so, some tried to escape or take over the ships. If they were overpowered, they were thrown overboard alive.

Brazil (by Portugal) in the 1880s. In some parts of the world it never quite stopped, however.

The effects on Africa of the slave trade were prolonged and devastating. The trade caused African to fight African as slave dealers fought for a share of the market. It destroyed the traditional pattern of African life and ruined the economy of many West African states and kingdoms. Slave labor made Europe and the Americas richer and Africa poorer.

Because of the slave trade, millions of men and women of African descent now live North and South America, the West Indies, and parts of Europe. The slaves brought their musical tradition with them, and their descendants adapted this legacy to produce the unique sound of jazz, blues, and reggae.

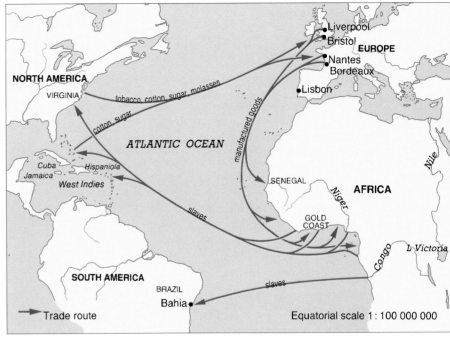

▲ At the height of the slave trade, there were three lines of trade: **Europe to Africa**—goods such as cotton cloth and firearms; **Africa to N. and S. America and the West Indies**—black slaves; **Americas to Europe**—raw goods (cotton, sugar, molasses, tobacco).

▼ A sale of estates, pictures, and African slaves in New Orleans, U.S., c. 1830.

**The African slave trade to the New World**

**16th century** Spain and Portugal begin trade in slaves.
**17th century** Development of plantation slavery by Dutch, French, British. Growth of the triangular slave trade (see map).
**Late 18th century** Opposition to slave trade starts.
**1807/1808** Slave trade made illegal in Great Britain and United States. Other European countries follow.
**1833** Slaves in all British possessions freed.
**1830–50** Arabs start new wave of slave trade in East Africa. Continues at least until 1870s.
**1861–65** American Civil War fought mainly over issue of slavery.
**1880s** Slavery abolished by most countries and slave trade dies out in the Americas.

# The Great Trek

FROM 1652 EMPLOYEES OF THE DUTCH EAST India Company, which dealt with trade between the Netherlands and its colonies in the Far East via Africa, began living at the Cape of Good Hope. Inland they knew of vast tracts of land that were sparsely populated by Africans.

Some of them began to move out of the small area that the company governed. Its administration let them take up vast areas of land for a very small fee, and soon they felt that this was their right. As numbers increased, the company was unable to control their actions or movements. As early as 1779 there was a small "war" between farmer settlers called Boers (Dutch for "farmer") and Africans.

## Dutch and British in conflict

At the end of the 18th century the Napoleonic Wars set European nations quarreling. In 1806, when the Cape became a British colony, British settlers joined the Dutch and French. The original Dutch settlers resented British rule, especially stricter laws about landholding and the treatment of African workers. (Slavery was abolished in the Cape Colony in 1828 and throughout the British Empire in 1833.) They

## Boers in South Africa

Although opened up for white settlement by the Boer trekkers (*Voortrekkers*), Natal was taken over by the British (1843), and did not become a Boer republic. All the Boer republics are now part of South Africa.

Swaziland and Lesotho became independent states in the 1960s and, although economically dependent on South Africa, have remained so.

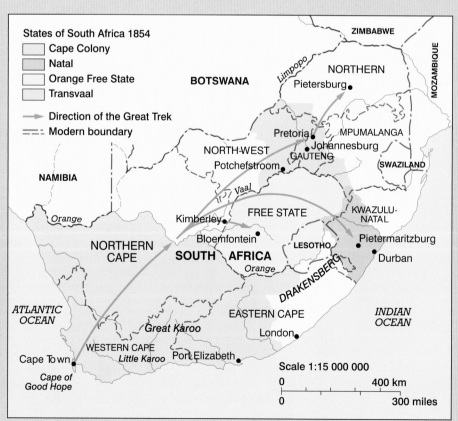

States of South Africa 1854
- Cape Colony
- Natal
- Orange Free State
- Transvaal

→ Direction of the Great Trek
═══ Modern boundary

ZIMBABWE
BOTSWANA
MOZAMBIQUE
NAMIBIA
Limpopo
NORTHERN
Pietersburg
Pretoria
MPUMALANGA
NORTH-WEST
Johannesburg
GAUTENG
Potchefstroom
SWAZILAND
Vaal
Orange
KWAZULU-NATAL
Kimberley
FREE STATE
Bloemfontein
Pietermaritzburg
NORTHERN CAPE
SOUTH AFRICA
LESOTHO
Durban
Orange
DRAKENSBERG
ATLANTIC OCEAN
EASTERN CAPE
INDIAN OCEAN
Great Karoo
London
WESTERN CAPE
Little Karoo
Port Elizabeth
Cape Town
Cape of Good Hope

Scale 1:15 000 000
0          400 km
0          300 miles

▶ After the Cape became a British colony in 1806, the Boers looked for new grazing lands. But for 625 miles (1,000 km) or so the Cape's hinterland is too dry for good cattle and sheep pasture. The pioneer Boers, the *Voortrekkers*, had seen good land beyond the Orange and Vaal Rivers. So the Boers of the Great Trek of 1836 turned their oxen teams to the high veld of the northeast.

Some went east instead of crossing the Vaal, going on into Natal. There they lost more than 400 men in fighting with the Zulu king Dingane and his warriors. Finally, in the battle of Blood River (December 1838) 3,000 Zulu died, with few Boer losses.

◄ When the Boer trekkers stopped at night, they arranged their camp with the ox wagons in a circle, or *laager*, within which they could keep their animals, cook, and sleep. They could defend themselves more easily in this makeshift fortress if they were attacked. The Boers' trek took them not into empty country but into land already used by the Bantu-speaking Xhosa, Sotho, and Zulu peoples, who were cattle keepers and farmers, just as they were.

wanted more land, and freedom to make their own laws. North and west of Cape Town the land was dry and barren. The best lands lay far to the northeast.

### The Boers trek northeast

Some pioneer Boers had already traveled ahead, in 1830. From 1835 Boers still in the south organized themselves into parties, and set out with their whole families and all their possessions in trek wagons drawn by teams of oxen.

There were many conflicts with Africans, for much of the best land was already being used by native Xhosa, Sotho, and Zulu farmers, who also had cattle. But dangers and hardships did not stop the Boers. They crossed the Vaal and Orange Rivers, and eventually formed two new Boer republics. These republics were called the Transvaal (1852) and the Orange Free State (1854).

### The Anglo-Boer War

At first almost all the Boers were cattle farmers. They were hard-working people, but life was difficult—especially in times of drought—for men, women, and young children too. They built simple houses out of local materials, and in many ways lived much like the Africans who were their neighbors.

The Boers were determined to keep their way of life separate from the British and African peoples, and kept strictly to the Calvinist teaching of the Dutch Reformed Church.

Later, gold and diamonds were found in the land that the Boers had settled, at Kimberley and around Johannesburg. Many outsiders came to work in the mines, which led to the development of mining shantytowns and deep Boer resentments.

This caused such difficulties that from 1899 to 1902 a war was fought between the Dutch settlers and their British rulers, which we remember as the Anglo-Boer War. It was a sad, bitter, and unnecessary war, and the memories left have caused much trouble ever since. It ended with a British victory, but in 1910 the British concluded a treaty that brought into being the Union of South Africa, uniting all the regions, including Transvaal and Orange Free State. Although they were under British rule, the Boers, known also as Afrikaners, became the dominant force in South Africa, and under their policies black people were denied voting rights until 1994.

# Exploration of the Interior

THE COURSE OF THE NILE THROUGH EGYPT had been known by Europeans for many hundreds of years. Western sailors had known the mouths of the Congo and Niger Rivers for more than 300 years. But in 1800 the routes of these great rivers were mostly unknown. Then, as European travelers began to move inland, the discovery of their sources became an obsession. So too did the hope of finding mineral wealth, particularly gold.

## The European scramble for Africa

In the 19th century steamships made traveling to ports in Africa easier. New medicines reduced the risk of fever. Missionaries wanted help in ending the slave trade. Some manufacturers wanted new markets, while others wanted raw materials. Some nations who had lost land in European wars wanted to gain land elsewhere. Once one nation took over a region, others wanted to follow. National rivalry and a desire to expand trade were the main reasons for government support of exploration, although many individual explorers often had other reasons.

## The search for the Nile's source

Ancient Greek and Roman geographers believed the Nile flowed down from the legendary snowcapped "Mountains of the Moon." British, French, Belgian,

and German explorers were all rivals in a quest to find the sources of the Blue and White Niles. The latter held the greater mystery. The maps available were no more than guesses, and evidence for the existence of the great East African lakes was based on ancient sources and confused accounts by traders and travelers. It was finally through the journeys of a number of British explorers that the courses of both Niles were established, ending 30 years of bitter dispute and wild "scientific" claims.

▼ Münster's woodcut map of Africa (1540) goes back to the map of Claudius Ptolemy (second century C.E.) and also draws on Arab and Portuguese sources. The Nile is shown emerging from the "Mountains of the Moon" in the far south; the upper Niger and its tributaries flow north—the wrong direction.

▼ Heinrich Barth (1821–65), a German, made two expeditions to Egypt in the 1840s, the first along the Nile. He led several British-sponsored expeditions into the northern regions of West Africa in the 1850s.

◄ Henry Morton Stanley (1841–1904), a Welsh-born American explorer, became famous when he "found" David Livingstone, the English missionary-explorer, at Ujiji in 1871. His various expeditions included crossing Africa from coast to coast. Kasulu, his young gun-bearer, was an ex-slave whom he adopted.

▶ Grant's drawing of Ripon Falls, Uganda, where the White Nile flows out of Lake Victoria. Several expeditions (1850s–70s) looked for the source of the Nile, including those of Richard Burton and J. H. Speke. It was not until after the death of Livingstone (1873) that Stanley was able to show that the White Nile flowed from Lake Victoria to Lake Albert before continuing north into Sudan.

▼ In 1875 by Lake Victoria, H. M. Stanley approaches the dwelling of the Kabaka (king) of Buganda, a nation of the Ganda people. Stanley wrote a famous letter about the Kabaka to the *Daily Telegraph* newspaper. This brought British and French missionaries, followed by British administrators, to Buganda (later a part of Uganda).

# Christian Missionaries in Africa

JESUS CHRIST LIVED AND DIED IN THE ROMAN province of Judea (present-day Israel). In the first 500 years after the death of Jesus Christ in Judea, Christian churches grew up in North Africa, Egypt, and Ethiopia. In the seventh century a new religion, Islam, came out of Arabia (see pages 32–33). The followers of its founder, Muhammad, destroyed the Christian churches of North Africa. Only those in Egypt and Ethiopia were left.

For nearly 1,000 years no followers of Christ (missionaries) went to Africa. But when, from the late 15th century onward, Portuguese sailors and then other European travelers started to explore along the coasts of Africa and later inland, missionaries followed them.

Sometimes missionaries themselves were the explorers. The first of them were Portuguese Catholic priests. They worked in parts of what are now the Democratic Republic of the Congo, Angola, and Mozambique. Where Dutch Protestant farmers settled at the Cape of Good Hope, they taught the local Africans about Christianity.

## The missionary movement

It was only from about the end of the 18th century that missions as we think of them today were established in Africa.

In 1737 Moravian (Czech) missionaries went to the Congo, followed later in the century by English, Dutch, and Germans. In West Africa Christianity was largely spread by freed African slaves, beginning in the late 18th century. One of the most important missionary orders was the Society of Missionaries of Africa (White Fathers), at first largely French, which was begun in Algeria in 1868. Italian Roman Catholics were active in Sudan, and Belgian ones in the Democratic Republic of the Congo.

Before long there were Protestant and Roman Catholic missionaries in nearly every part of Africa. As well as preaching, they founded schools and hospitals and, depending on one's point of view, interfered with traditional cultural habits.

## Christianity in Africa today

As African churches grew, African Christians were trained as pastors and priests, and in time became the leaders of the churches. They have also started their own churches. Since widespread African independence in the 1960s, there are now far fewer missionaries in Africa from overseas—Africans themselves are more often the missionaries.

▶ A Yoruba (Nigerian) woodworker has carved the baptism of Jesus on this font. It is in the form of a traditional drum.

▼ Some African Christians have begun their own churches, where they practice healing the sick by prayer. Here, a priest lays hands on a young woman to cast out the evil spirit which possesses her and causes her illness.

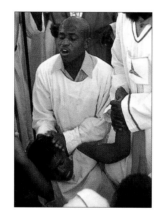

▶ Christians, black and white, receive Holy Communion in a church in Nairobi, Kenya.

▼ The style of this cross from the Democratic Republic of the Congo dates back to the Portuguese missionaries at the end of the 15th century.

Mediterranean Sea

**Main European missions, 15th–19th centuries**

**15th–18th centuries** Portuguese Catholic missionaries in Angola, Republic of Congo, Mozambique, Mombasa.

**1737** Protestant Moravian Brethren to southern Africa.
**1799** Protestant London Missionary Society to southern Africa.
**1804** Anglican Church Missionary Society (CMS) to Sierra Leone.
**1845** CMS in Nigeria. **1864** Samuel Crowther, first African bishop.
**1868** Catholic White Fathers in Algeria. **1877, 1879** CMS and Catholic White Fathers in Buganda.

1883
1859
1840
1881
1873
1881
1840
TUNISIA
1872
1884
1891
1843
1892
1879

MOROCCO

ALGERIA

LIBYA

1854
1882

EGYPT

Nile

1861

Red Sea

WESTERN
SAHARA
(MOROCCO)

MAURITANIA

MALI

NIGER

CHAD

L Chad

SUDAN

1900
1899
1899
1839
ERITREA

1863
DJIBOUTI

1846
SENEGAL
1821
GAMBIA
GUINEA-
BISSAU

GUINEA

BURKINA
FASO

BENIN

NIGERIA

1903
1900

ETHIOPIA

SIERRA
LEONE
1804
1808
1836
LIBERIA
1833

CÔTE
D'IVOIRE

1913
GHANA
TOGO

1834

1842

1857

CENTRAL AFRICAN
REPUBLIC

1913

1906

SOMALIA

CAMEROON
1845

EQUATORIAL
GUINEA

L Turkana

UGANDA
1879
1877

1910
KENYA

SÃO TOMÉ &
PRÍNCIPE

1848
1842
1887

1854
GABON
1874

CONGO
(R.O.)

Congo

RWANDA
BURUNDI

L Victoria

1844

1873
1878

1883
1882

CONGO
(D.R.O.)

TANZANIA

L Tanganyika

INDIAN
OCEAN

— · — Modern boundary

Muslim area

Advance of Christian missionaries

Protestant mission with date of foundation

Catholic mission with date of foundation

1866
1879

1885

1881

ANGOLA

1888

1876
1869
1863

1881
MALAWI
1888

L Malawi

COMOROS

1886

ZAMBIA

1876

ATLANTIC
OCEAN

1879

1886

ZIMBABWE

MOZAMBIQUE

1864
MADAGASCAR
1820

1867

► Reflecting the diversity of missionary teachings, the Christian churches are represented by many different denominations. The so-called independent churches are strongest in the Democratic Republic of the Congo, Kenya, Ghana, Nigeria, Zimbabwe, and South Africa. Since the seventh century C.E. Islam has dominated North Africa, Somalia, and northern Sudan. Traditional religions have little following in these areas.

NAMIBIA

1847

BOTSWANA

Limpopo

Zambezi

SWAZILAND

SOUTH AFRICA

Orange

LESOTHO

1816

1799
1801

1823

1737

Scale 1:34 000 000

0                    1500 km

0          1000 miles

# Islam in Africa

T HE PROPHET MUHAMMAD, FOUNDER OF Islam, was born in Arabia about 570 C.E. and died in 632. Arabian Bedouin tribes had joined him in his community, and an Islamic state had been formed. After his death his disciples, using the holy book of his writings, the Koran (*Qur'an*) and his sayings (*Hadith*), put together the Holy Law (*Shari'a*). Assisted by Arabian armies, they extended their control over neighboring tribes and communities.

By 640 they controlled Syria and Palestine to the north, including Jerusalem. In 642 Alexandria was occupied, and in 697, Carthage. Within 100 years the peoples of the North African coast, and many of the nomadic tribes of the interior, were Muslim.

The old Christian churches disappeared, although Christians and Jews, who were "people of the Book," and who, like Muslims, worshiped one god, were not forced to convert. But they had to pay a special tax. They also experienced periodic persecution and slowly, over the years, many came to accept Islam. Christian churches survived only in Egypt (see pages 56–57) and Ethiopia and, for a few centuries, in Nubia (see pages 74–75).

## Islam south of the Sahara

Although the first Islamic expansion in Africa came about through military conquest, since then it has usually been through trade. Muslim immigrants taught other peoples by faithfully observing their religious practices. Islam has not usually sent out special missionaries in the way that Christianity has—religious teachers came only after a Muslim community was formed.

Islam began to spread south into West Africa with the trans-Saharan Arab-Berber camel caravans, perhaps as early as the ninth century. By the 11th century it was widespread in the region and became the official religion of the great kingdoms of Ghana, Mali, Songhay, and Kanem-Borno.

Along the coasts and islands of East Africa Islam was brought by sailors and merchants from the Middle East who settled there. The Somali tribes of the Horn of Africa and peoples of northern Sudan and Ethiopia took up Islam through contacts with Arabia and Egypt, to their east and north.

Only in the 19th and 20th centuries did Islam expand widely in areas south of the Sahara. Even today, outside the almost totally Islamic nations (Morocco, Tunisia, Algeria, Mauritania, Mali, and Niger, for example), Islam is very much an urban religion. This is especially true in East and central

▲ Mosques adapt to local building styles. This mosque at Timbuktu has been built from poles and mud, constructed so cleverly that the building can withstand the rare but very heavy rain. In this building, as in the most ornate or the most simple mosque, the basic rules are the same: the *mihrab*, or niche, to indicate the direction of Mecca, and the *minbar* for the Friday sermon.

◄ The domed mosque stands in a cloistered courtyard used as a school (*madrassah*) where pupils are instructed in the Koran and the *Shari'a*. Beyond is a narrow courtyard, and near the main entrance is a minaret, from which the call to prayer goes out five times a day. In a city like Cairo with several mosques, the largest would become the Assembly Mosque where the special Friday prayers are made.

Africa. Only in Tanzania are there areas where, in the late 19th and early 20th centuries, whole rural populations adopted Islam as their religion.

### The command to prayer

One of the special commandments of faithful Muslims is the law to pray every day. There are two kinds of prayer (or *salat* in Arabic). Private, personal prayer can take place anywhere at any time. But Prophet Muhammad also ordered Muslims to pray publicly, five times a day, reciting special prayers while standing or kneeling in certain ways. Believers must also "wash" their hands, feet, and face (with water or dry sand) before praying.

These prayers do not need to be made at a mosque. Wherever a Muslim is, he spreads his prayer mat and turns in the direction of Mecca. (Mecca, inland from the Red Sea in Saudi Arabia, is where Muhammad was born.) But on Fridays, the special day in the Muslim week, believers go to the mosque.

A mosque is not used for ceremonies such as weddings and funerals. Instead, they are held in the home. In the beginning, all a mosque needed to be was a place to meet, with water for washing. But over the years some features were added. Most mosques now have a tower, a minaret, from which the mosque official (the *muezzin*) calls Muslims to prayer (at sunrise, noon, mid-afternoon, sunset, and two hours after sunset). These beautiful musical calls to the faithful are known as *adhan*.

# Africa's Religions

OVER THE WHOLE OF AFRICA THERE ARE roughly the same number of Christians as Muslims—about 85 percent of Africans in total. The founders of these two religions, Jesus and Muhammad, lived in lands close to Africa. Both religions spread into North Africa and Ethiopia. In this country there has also been a community of Jews. So for many North Africans either Islam or Christianity is their traditional religion.

## Traditional religions

A "traditional religion" is usually taken to mean that followed by a particular group of people. Before the European colonial era, traditional religions were followed by most Africans outside North Africa, Ethiopia, and many coastal settlements in East Africa. Now, about 13 percent of people follow them.

These religions have no mosques, churches, or temples. But very often there are special places, perhaps on top of a hill or under a large tree, where people gather to pray to the gods and spirits, and to offer gifts to them. Often an important person in the society, such as an elderly man or woman, acts as the priest, leading the ceremony and communicating with the "spirits," or ancestors.

In some places goats, cows, or chickens are sacrificed. Sometimes offerings of cooked food and beer are made. A tiny house for the spirits may be built in each family's courtyard, where food is placed (see also pages 62–63).

## Gods and spirits

Old people tell the children stories about the gods and how they want people to live. Many people believe in one god, a "high god," who lives in the sky and who was the creator of the world. Many also believe that there are spirits in trees, rivers, mountains, living creatures, and all around the village. If there is illness or bad luck, it is often thought that it is because someone has done a wrong deed and made one of the spirits angry. Therefore good relations among the members of a family and between neighbors are valued highly.

## Ceremony and everyday religion

People believe that the spirits of the dead, especially those who have died recently, are still near them, and food and drink offerings are made to keep those spirits happy. When a new baby is born it may be given the name of someone who has just died. At the time of a funeral special prayers and gifts for the

◀ A traditional healer has been called to help a sick woman in northern Cameroon. Her family watch while the healer performs a ritual as the patient lies quietly on a mat.

◀ Carving of Shango, voice and power of thunder, who was once king of Oyo. The Yoruba people revere him as a god and there are many shrines to him. Only his priests arrange burial of people struck by lightning.

▼ In Ghana a family gathers in their courtyard to make a sacrifice of one of their animals—to please and show respect for their god and the spirits of their ancestors. The sacrifice is conducted by the clan head or, in some cults, a professional priest.

▶ The Faron Mosque in Khartoum, capital of Sudan, which lies at the confluence, or meeting place, of the White and Blue Niles. This is the minaret from which the call to prayer goes out five times each day.

Khartoum was an Egyptian garrison town in the 1820s. It was here that the British soldier, General Gordon, met his death after a famous siege in 1885.

spirit of the dead person may be offered. These spirits are considered to be ancestors and are always treated with enormous respect, and even feared.

Other times when special prayers and offerings are made to the spirits are at the birth of a child, at weddings, and at initiation rites (when boys and girls are accepted as grown-up people in their society). In other parts of the world, too, it is after births and deaths, and for marriages, that people most often go to a church, synagogue, chapel, or mosque.

### "Witch doctors" and healing

You often hear the words "witch doctor" and "medicine man" when people talk about African religion. Some people think that they are evil people, but in fact they often are healers or fortune tellers, and they are considered to be extremely important.

When people are puzzled about the cause of illness or bad fortune, the witch doctor tries to find the answer so that people can get rid of the evil that caused trouble. This might be done by entering into a trance to communicate with ancestral spirits in the "spirit world." Although it is believed that witch doctors have the power to harm people, they are much more often viewed as highly trained religious specialists and are revered for their abilities to predict events, to make rain, and to heal the sick.

▼ The Friday Mosque at Mopti, southern Mali, near the Niger River is on an ancient caravan route. Local materials and traditional methods were used to create this truly African mosque.

Strict Muslims should pray five times every day wherever they are, but on Fridays should do so with others at a large mosque.

Women are not forbidden to attend mosque prayers, but generally they pray at home.

# Distribution of People in Africa

THE POPULATION OF ANY PARTICULAR country or region within a country depends on such factors as physical environment, the country's history, and the economic conditions.

## Sparse and dense populations

It is not surprising that desert areas and very mountainous regions usually have low populations. The deserts of Namibia and the vast Sahara—at 3 million sq miles (7.7 million sq. km) it is almost the size of the United States)—support very few people. The same is true of high mountains, but the fertile foothills surrounding the mountains often attract dense rural populations, as in East Africa and west central Africa.

Dense populations are usually found along rivers, (such as the Nile) or around lakes (for example, Lake Victoria), which provide food as well as water. In several parts of Africa—the coasts of North Africa, along the Niger River in West Africa, in Egypt, and in Sudan—large cities have existed for many thousands of years, and these cities continue to grow. But even today, most of Africa's 500 million or more people live in the countryside, in villages, and in small towns that are market centers.

## The growth of modern cities

The existence of minerals (as in the Democratic Republic of the Congo, Zambia, and South Africa) led in the 20th century to the rapid growth of several large industrial cities, which attract yet more people. More than 50 million Africans now live in large cities, compared with only 7 million in the 1920s. Because of overcrowding and poverty, people often live in shantytowns where they have no proper gas, electricity, or water supplies.

◄ Johannesburg (founded 1886) is the commercial and major manufacturing center of South Africa with a population of more than 3 million. Far inland, the city developed around gold-mining sites. Its center looks like that of modern European or American cities.

► Xhosa men outside their huts in contemporary South Africa. The isolated village is still home to a very large number of Africans.

Early contact between white colonists and the Xhosa people led to conflict over control of Xhosa land. Nine wars were fought between 1779 and 1878.

## Growth of African cities from 1300 C.E.

**By 1300** Cairo, with 500,000 people, bigger than any metropolis in Europe or the Middle East.

**By 1690** Tunis established near the ancient city of Carthage and grew rapidly under Muslim rule.

**1800s** In West Africa, trading towns such as Lagos, Kano, Sokoto, and Ibadan grow to population sizes of 20,000–100,000.

**1880s** Establishment of European colonial towns and administrative capitals—Kinshasa (1881), Brazzaville (1883), Dar es Salaam (1885), and Kampala (1890).

**1910** Cape Town, the earliest European city, becomes capital of South Africa. (Population today more than 2.9 million.)

▶ The largest cities in Africa today are in Nigeria, South Africa, Egypt, Morocco, and Algeria. Ethiopia has a large population but little city development. Gabon and Namibia have small populations but great urbanization.

- City with over 3 million people

Population per sq mi
- 260
- 130
- 26

Scale 1:62 000 000

0 _____ 1500 km
0 _____ 1000 miles

▶ The Sultan of Agades within a courtyard of his palace. The dried mud walls are built on a wooden framework and have been in constant repair since the palace was first put up in the 14th century. Agades is an oasis city in the Sahara region of northern Niger. Throughout Africa, oases— the sites of springs or wells in deserts—are the centers of dense rural populations.

# African Peoples and Languages

WHAT DO THE PEOPLE OF AFRICA LOOK like? And what languages do they speak? Each person is an individual, but there are some features that are typical of most Africans.

## Peoples of Africa

Almost everywhere in Africa, native people have dark brown or black hair, and black, brown, or yellowish brown skins. All have brown eyes. It is the dark hair and skin color that gave us the word Negro, from the Latin *niger*, which means black.

In the north, along the Mediterranean coast, most people are not very different from the Greeks, Italians, and Spaniards on the north shores, with straight or wavy hair and brown skin. This shows their common ancestry. In Ethiopia and Somalia there are also people with light brown skin and wavy hair, and often sharply pointed noses.

In general, as one travels south, the people are darker with flatter noses and with hair so strongly curled that it is called spiraled. Some are very tall, for example, the Dinka of Sudan, or the Tutsi of Rwanda and Burundi. Some, such as the Mbuti people of the Democratic Republic of the Congo, are very short.

In southern Africa there are people of different appearance. They are the Khoekhoe ("Hottentots"), who were herders and hunters, and the San (or "Bushmen") peoples, who were hunter-gatherers. Both have yellowish brown skin, softer hair, and epicanthic (long) eye folds like most east Asians. The San are much shorter than the Khoekhoe but taller than the Mbuti.

All along the East African coast there are people with lighter skin and straighter hair than the inland people. Their ancestors were both Arab and African.

## Languages

Today Africa is home to about 1,800 languages, grouped into four different language "families": "Afroasiatic" languages are spoken in North and northeastern Africa, and as far south as Kenya. "Niger-Congo," the largest language family, includes most of the languages of West, East, central, and southern Africa. The "Nilo-Saharan" languages are spoken in Sudan and in East Africa. The "Khoisan" languages, with their "click" sounds, are mostly spoken in southern Africa.

The names used for the families give some idea of the part of Africa in which they are spoken. Within each family the separate languages are related, sharing vocabulary and grammatical systems.

▲ A Kabyle man from Algeria, where Arabic is now spoken. The old Berber and Semitic languages survive only in remote rural areas.

▲ A Coptic girl from Egypt, where Arabic is now the first language. Copts are descendants of ancient Egypt who took up the Christian faith.

▲ In northern Sudan Arabic is the usual language today. This woman comes from Omdurman, a city on the Nile near Khartoum.

▼ The four major language families of Africa are shown on this map. **1. Afroasiatic family** which includes Hebrew and Arabic. It is clear that these languages, and the people who first spoke them, are linked with languages and peoples outside Africa. Arabic, most widely spoken, was introduced only after the Islamic invasions of the seventh century C.E. onward. **2. Khoisan languages** spoken by the Khoekhoe (Hottentots) and the San ("Bushmen"). **3. Nilo-Saharan** and **4. Niger-Congo.** These contain the languages spoken by people who are traditionally thought of as African, with dark brown skin and eyes, and spiraled hair.

Language families (including two non-African families)
- ☐ Niger-Congo
- ☐ Nilo-Saharan
- ☐ Afroasiatic
- ☐ Khoisan
- ☐ Austronesian-Malagasy
- ☐ English and Afrikaans with indigenous Bantu

—— Bantu line
Igbo Separate language

Scale 1 : 62 000 000

0 ——————— 1500 km
0 ——————— 1000 miles

▲ This Baulé girl from Côte d'Ivoire speaks an Akan language related to Asante and Fanti (Ghanaian languages of the Niger-Congo family).

▲ Some sounds in the Khoisan "click" language spoken by this San girl from Botswana have been adopted by Xhosa and Zulu languages.

▲ Like most peoples from southern West Africa to South Africa and Kenya, this Mozambiquan man speaks a Bantu language (Niger-Congo family).

▲ A young man of Karamoja, northern Uganda, who speaks the language Karamajong of the Nilo-Saharan family. It is closely related to languages spoken in the southern parts of Sudan and in Tanzania and Kenya, such as those used by Maasai and Samburu groups.

▲ In Ganvie, southern Benin, the local people have built houses raised on stilts in the lagoon. They use dugout canoes for getting about and transporting goods. They speak Akan like the Baulé people (see above), a Niger-Congo language of the coastal regions of West Africa.

On the island of Madagascar, where the population is chiefly related to Indonesia, not to the African mainland, the languages belong to a fifth type, known as Austronesian.

### A widely spoken African language

Swahili is a well-known African language. It is the "mother tongue" of people along the East African coast from southern Somalia to northern Mozambique (including Kenya, Tanzania, Uganda, Rwanda, and Burundi) and is also spoken by traders over most of East Africa.

Swahili (or more correctly, Kiswahili) is placed in the Niger-Congo subgroup known as Bantu. This name was chosen when a scholar found that in many languages (spoken from west central Africa across to East Africa and down to the Cape of Good Hope) there was a word resembling *bantu* that meant "people." In Kiswahili the word is *watu*. He found that Bantu languages have many shared features.

Kiswahili has a rich vocabulary containing many words derived from Arabic as well as some from Indian languages, Persian, Portuguese, and English. And English now borrows words from Kiswahili. *Safari* is a Swahili word meaning journey, and comes from the Arabic *safara* (travel).

Other well-known Bantu languages include Zulu, the Shona language that is widely spoken in Zimbabwe, and Bemba, the language of millions of people living in Zambia.

Today all over Africa European languages are learned as a second language. The most common are English and French; others are Portuguese and Spanish. In South Africa the local form of Dutch is known as Afrikaans.

# Education and Literacy

WHEN WE THINK OF EDUCATION, WE usually think of schools. In most of Africa there have been schools, in the usual sense of permanent places of learning, only for a short time. And it is true that literacy—being able to read and write—has only recently arrived. But this does not mean that there was no education previously, nor does it mean that, because there were no books, people in Africa did not remember the stories of the past or their history.

## Islamic schools

Before Western contact, the only written languages were Arabic (in North Africa and parts of East and

◀ A Muslim teacher instructs his class at their evening school in a street in Kano, Nigeria. The pupils use wooden writing boards. Instruction in the Koran for boys is the main object of these Muslim schools. During the daytime boys and girls receive more formal education in schools run by the government.

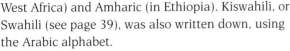

West Africa) and Amharic (in Ethiopia). Kiswahili, or Swahili (see page 39), was also written down, using the Arabic alphabet.

Wherever there were Muslims, there were Koranic schools where boys could learn Arabic in order to read the Koran. This is the sacred book of Islam "given" by God to the prophet Muhammad. Unlike the Bible, the Koran is supposed to be read in its original language.

Koranic schools continue, and many children (nowadays both boys and girls) attend such a school in the evening after going to a regular school during the day. There are also Islamic universities, including the world's oldest university, al-Azhar, in Cairo, founded in 988 B.C.E.

## Missions and education

Wherever Western Christian missionaries went in Africa, their first task was to write down the local language, to learn it, and to translate the Bible and other religious books. Then they could teach new Christians to read and write. In fact, baptism was often not allowed until a person was literate, and the common word for a Christian was "a reader."

The first "bush schools" were very simple, and often the church and the school shared the same building. Because the area served by the schools was extremely large, pupils often had to travel long distances. More advanced schools were therefore usually begun as boarding schools, and up to the present many children still board, at least for their secondary education.

## Traditional education

African boys and girls in the past used to learn the skills that were necessary for their lives and livelihoods from their parents and families. Particular skills, for example, metalworking and pottery, could be passed on to sons and daughters.

Many African societies also had special separate "camps" for boys and girls, which they would go to when they were ready to be accepted as adults by the rest of the community. There the male elders taught the boys, and older women taught the girls—about marriage, social customs, the society's rules, and its responsibilities and punishments.

Some of the teaching was given in the form of proverbs, stories, and songs. The history of each community was also remembered through stories and songs passed down from generation to generation. This is called oral history.

◀ At a "bush school" for young Dinka boys in southern Sudan, the pupils wear a simple uniform. The school building is of basic construction, and the children sit on rough-cut wooden benches. Their teacher stands at the front of the class and instructs in a traditional Western fashion.

## Modern and adult education

Today all over Africa there are primary and secondary schools very much like those in Europe and North America. But not all children are able to go to school, and usually fewer girls than boys are taught. Major obstacles to education include poverty, overcrowding, slow economic development, and the pandemic disease HIV/AIDS. However, in many countries most children attend primary school. Fewer children are able to continue at a secondary school.

Those who attend secondary schools may later attend universities or colleges of technology. African students usually learn at least one European language—mainly French or English, but also others

▲ These Xhosa boys are taking part in a ceremony for their initiation as adults. The Xhosa of South Africa, like many other peoples, have camps for the youths to prepare them for joining the adult community. This is still an important part of village life even though many adult Xhosa now work for much of the time in industrial and urban centers such as Port Elizabeth, St. Croix, Durban, and East London.

depending on their country's colonial background—as well as one or more of the local languages.

Because most adults could not attend school as children, today in many parts of Africa short daily classes are arranged to teach them to read and write their own languages. If they are able to attend regularly, adults can usually learn to read well in just a few months.

Population growth works against the efforts being made to reduce illiteracy. Another problem is that adults do not always have opportunities to practice reading and writing, and so their skills do not become permanent. Rates of illiteracy among women are always higher—sometimes two to three times higher—than among men.

# African Art

AFRICANS OFTEN DECORATE THE EVERYDAY objects they use in their homes, such as plates and bowls. They also make objects used in worship that are valued for their appearance. In some societies (mainly those that have kings or chiefs) objects such as heads or figures of people or animals are made for their appearance alone.

## The earliest African art

Although today people are most familiar with carvings and sculpture, the earliest African art forms known are the paintings and engravings on smooth rock that survive in caves, rock shelters, and even on open boulders. Thousands have been found in the central Sahara, and there are many more in southern and south central Africa.

Rock art had profound religious importance to the peoples who produced it, and many scenes are probably visions of the spirit world. Wild and, later on, domestic animals were the most common subjects, although humans, everyday objects, and even bizarre otherworldly creatures were depicted.

The oldest rock painting in Africa (c.25,000 B.C.E.) comes from the Apollo 11 Cave in Namibia, southern Africa. Southern Africa has also produced the oldest art anywhere in the world—a piece of geometrically engraved red ocher (hematite) and 41 shell beads were found in Blombos Cave on the south coast of South Africa, all dating to about 73,000 B.C.E.

## African sculpture and carving

The earliest sculptures (outside of Egypt) known in Africa are baked clay (terra-cotta) heads found around the modern village of Nok in northern Nigeria. They show heads and figures of humans and animals, and are dated to about 2,000 years ago. The Nok tradition of sculpture in clay influences the art of the Yoruba people centuries later. Clay figures are less common than carved wood, which is found wherever there are forests. Drums, with carved bodies made from tree trunks, are another art form.

Objects used in the homes of kings and chiefs— stools, chairs, headrests, bowls, cups—are very finely carved and decorated. Ivory (from elephants' tusks) and bone were also carved and used for smaller objects, such as spoons, small dishes, or bracelets.

In some parts of Africa utensils and figures are carved from soapstone, a very soft stone. A few ancient peoples learned to use metals, such as bronze, to make objects. They were very valuable and mainly for rulers or for use in religious ceremonies.

◀ At just 8 in (20 cm) high, this is not a stool, but a headrest! The Luba women of the Democratic Republic of the Congo arrange their hair elaborately (like the women in the carving) and use carved headrests at night to protect their hairstyles. Some are made of ivory; this one is carved from wood. As well as using them at night, the Luba also use these headrests in a kind of divination or fortune-telling.

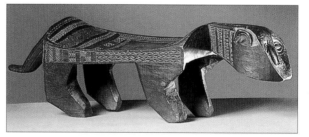

◀ A headrest in animal form from the Ngindo people, southwest Tanzania. In many societies the men wear elaborate hairstyles, fixed with mud and fibers. Often they carry the headrest on a cord around their neck.

▶ The Baulé people of Côte d'Ivoire are well known for their realistic sculpture. This figure of a bearded old man is carved with great attention to detail. Note the intricate hairstyle and the gentle expression.

▼ Calabashes, or gourds, are the fruit of a vine, and grow widely in Africa. When cut and dried, they are used as measures, serving dishes, containers, and sound boxes for musical instruments. Long thin ones are used as bottles. These gourds from Nigeria have been carved with a sharp tool and dyed.

## African masks

In many parts of Africa members of secret societies used masks in dances at their ceremonies. These masks make up some of the most striking art in all Africa. They were sometimes carved in wood and painted, or made of skin stretched over a wooden frame. Long robes of cloth, or of grass or raffia, might hang from them and cover the whole of the wearer's body to frighten the watchers.

## Everyday decorative art

Baskets are woven everywhere in Africa, and they are often beautifully decorated. Food containers and trays are carved; stools are decorated with beads and wire hammered in patterns. Earrings, necklaces, and bracelets made of metal, wood, or beads are valued for their beauty. Sometimes the walls of mud houses are used like an artist's canvas and covered with drawings and paintings.

Where cloth is woven, it is often decorated in the process of weaving, with colored yarn used in patterns. Plain cloth is decorated by "painting on" an image or pattern in wax and then dyeing the cloth. The wax prevents the dye from seeping into the cloth, so that the image stays in the original cloth color while surrounding material takes up the dye.

African art is essentially a community art, hence the everyday decorative art. Only in recent years have individual artists become recognized.

### Indigo dyeing

In Nigeria, Côte d'Ivoire, Senegal, and Madagascar certain plants are grown for a blue dye, indigo. Their crushed leaves are formed into balls. The blue dye is produced when the balls are soaked in an alkaline solution, made from the ash of green wood. This also "sets" the dye, to make the cloth colorfast.

Woven fabric, or skeins of cotton yarn, can now be dipped in the cold dye. The cloth or yarn is redipped several times until the right shade of blue is obtained. In Kano, northern Nigeria, the dyeing is done in vats set in the ground (left).

# Music and Dance

ALL OVER AFRICA MUSIC IS A VALUED PART of daily life. Music is made by the singing voice and by musical instruments. And with music goes dancing, because to Africans the art of music is also the art of moving to music.

## What are the instruments used?

Musical instruments in Africa vary depending on the materials and skills that are available. Drums are common and are usually made by stretching an animal skin over a hollowed-out tree trunk. Where trees are unavailable, clay pots may be used. Other percussion instruments include bells, xylophones, and the "thumb piano," *likembe*.

Flutes, trumpets, and other wind instruments are made from wood, reeds, or metal. Stringed instruments are often made using gourds (fruits) for the sound boxes. Even a hunting bow can become a kind of violin.

In societies where there is a king or a chief, he may have at his court an orchestra, with a singer who sings special "praise songs" in his honor. In these societies solo players of instruments may also be found, but usually in Africa everyone joins in music and dance.

▲ A portable xylophone, used in Cameroon, probably has its origins in the Republic of Congo, to the south.

▶ The *likembe*, "thumb piano," may come from the Democratic Republic of the Congo, but has spread south to Angola, Zambia, and South Africa, and east to Uganda.

◀ At the court of the emir of Zaria (northern Nigeria), an orchestra plays, while the drummer sings songs in praise of the emir.

▼ In southern Angola a hunting bow with brace added becomes a musical instrument and is played with the mouth.

▲ This late 17th-century bronze plaque from Benin, West Africa, depicts royal-court drummers.

▶ Dancers of the masked society, *awa*, among the Dogon of Mali. They dance at funerals, telling myths of life and death.

▲ A masked figure from Sierra Leone, appearing in a dance of the men's society, *bondo*.

▲ A masked figure makes an appearance at the Ogun festival of the Yoruba.

Modern popular African music, as played on radio throughout the continent, has traditional roots but uses modern (Western) instruments.

## Singing at work and at play

Many African songs are work songs, sung while the soil is hoed, while grain is ground into flour, or the oars in a boat are pulled. A leader will sing a verse; others will take up a chorus. Children have all kinds of singing games, with clapping and jumping.

American and European pop music, jazz, rhythm and blues, reggae, and hip hop have all been strongly influenced by traditional African music taken by slaves to the Americas.

## The time of the full moon

Moonlit nights are the time for dancing in African villages. When the drums beat, people gather to dance in open spaces. The dancers often wear bells and rattles at their ankles and knees. Among some peoples in West Africa and west central Africa, there are the special masked societies, whose members dance wearing masks and costumes, while others watch. Dances are often religious, and are performed to heal people and to encourage group solidarity.

# Houses

ALL OVER AFRICA—EXCEPT FOR THE EAST coast cities—Africans traditionally built their homes from earth, wood, and grass, and sometimes animal hides and skins. Houses built in these materials do not last long. Such houses are still being built, although stones and bricks, with cement and iron, are now used. The house may be in a village or town, or isolated in farmland.

## Traditional rooms and compounds

African houses are not usually divided into rooms, although occasionally very simple partitions are used. Each building is used for one purpose, so if another room is needed, another separate house is added. Several houses are grouped about an open space or courtyard, which becomes an open-air room where much of the daily activity goes on.

The head of the family usually has his own room. Small children mostly sleep with their mothers, and the older unmarried girls sleep in the room of their mother or grandmother. The young unmarried men generally have their own sleeping house, sometimes right away from the rest of the family.

If there is a kitchen, it is used mainly as a storeroom—except during the rains, cooking is

▲ The Sarwa, millet farmers of Chad in west central Africa, live in villages made up of walled compounds, each of which contains one or more quite separate houses. There are narrow paths between the compound walls. The open courtyards are fenced with walls like those of the houses – either of sunbaked mud or of sorghum stalks. Here, grain and water are stored in large pots; firewood is stacked against the walls; meals are prepared out in the open.

▲ The Nuba people who live in the hills of southern Kordofan (Sudan) build their thatched houses in a ring pattern. Clay walls link the houses to form a courtyard, which has a single exit and onto which the houses open.

▶ The compounds of the Nupe are built on fertile plains near the Niger River in central Nigeria. Each adult member of the family has a separate house. The granaries are raised on stones and there is an outer enclosing wall.

◀ A Nubian stands outside his main door. Animal and geometric patterns are drawn into the plaster, but human figures do not feature at all, since the Nubians are Muslims, who frown upon representations of people.

▲ The Asante of southern Ghana build rectangular houses, joined with short walls to form a compound. Complicated relief patterns are drawn in the plaster. The courtyard side of the room is often open to the air.

done outside. In most compounds there will be separate storehouses for grains and vegetables.

## Building a house

Although similar materials are used all over Africa, there are many different styles and shapes, including round, square, and rectangular.

The most common building method is to set straight slender tree trunks in the shape wanted, and attach a framework made of thinner more flexible poles. Then earth and water are trampled into mud in a pit, which is used to fill up the framework. This method, which is called wattle and daub, has been used by peoples all over the world.

The framework for the roof is put together on the ground before it is lifted into place, and covered with bunches of thatching grass. There are probably no windows, and just one small opening for a door. Later, the walls may be plastered with special earth, and the floor polished by applying mud mixed with cow dung, which gives a handsome finish.

Commonly when rural people move to cities they can only afford to live in shantytowns, where shack houses are put together from odd bits of timber and corrugated iron.

# Husuni Kubwa

EW OLD BUILDINGS HAVE SURVIVED IN Africa because the materials (earth, wood, and grass) do not last. But on the east coast, under the influence of Arab immigrants, buildings were made of more permanent materials.

Some of them survived and in recent years have been excavated. They reveal much about the unique East coast culture, which was both Islamic and African in origin.

## With what, and how, did they build?

The Arab and African architects and builders used coral from the sea. Soft at first, this cut easily into building blocks that hardened in time. It was also ground and burned to make mortar. Ground coral was used for plastering, and small pieces, known as coral rag, were used to fill in walls. The width of the rooms was limited by the length of the rafters. They used mangrove poles, about 8 feet (2.4 m) long. Rooms were therefore either 8 foot (2.4 m) square or long and narrow.

## Husuni Kubwa

One of the most interesting groups of buildings on the coast is that at Kilwa, on a headland just outside the modern town. (Kilwa is l25 miles/40 km south of Dar es Salaam, in Tanzania.) The meaning of Husuni Kubwa is "large fortified house," and it was used as the home and palace of the local Muslim ruler, Sultan al-Hasan ibn Sulaiman.

Husuni Kubwa is a group of pavilions set around courtyards, on a slope. There are public and private rooms, storerooms, an octagonal pool, and a small mosque separate from the rest but connected by a staircase. The buildings were beautifully decorated with elaborately carved coral panels. There is an outer wall that seems to be part of a fortification.

Kilwa flourished in the 14th century, and one inscription that has been found in the building names a sultan of that time. In the 15th century Kilwa declined in importance, and the ruler moved away into the town.

▶ A reconstruction and ground plan of Husuni Kubwa, showing the private rooms and courtyards on the headland as well as the octagonal bathing pool, the palace courtyard, and, beyond it, the business courtyard surrounded by storerooms and with its own decorative pool. Local sail-boats called dhows brought visitors and traders to the palace from ports along the east coast of Africa and Asia.

# Part Two

# A Regional Guide to Africa

▲ A mask of the Dan people, Liberia.

▶ A camel caravan at rest, seen from a hot-air balloon, at Bilma Oasis, Niger.

**Inset** Key to maps in this section of the book.

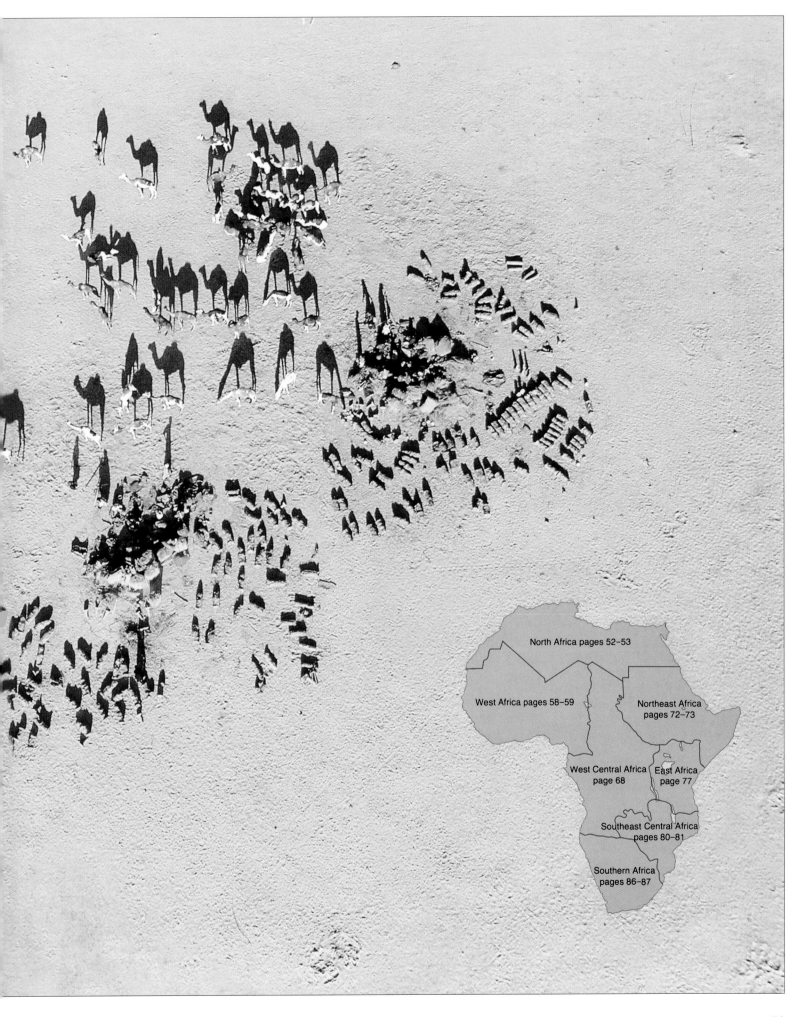

North Africa pages 52–53

West Africa pages 58–59

Northeast Africa
pages 72–73

West Central Africa
page 68

East Africa
page 77

Southeast Central Africa
pages 80–81

Southern Africa
pages 86–87

# North Africa

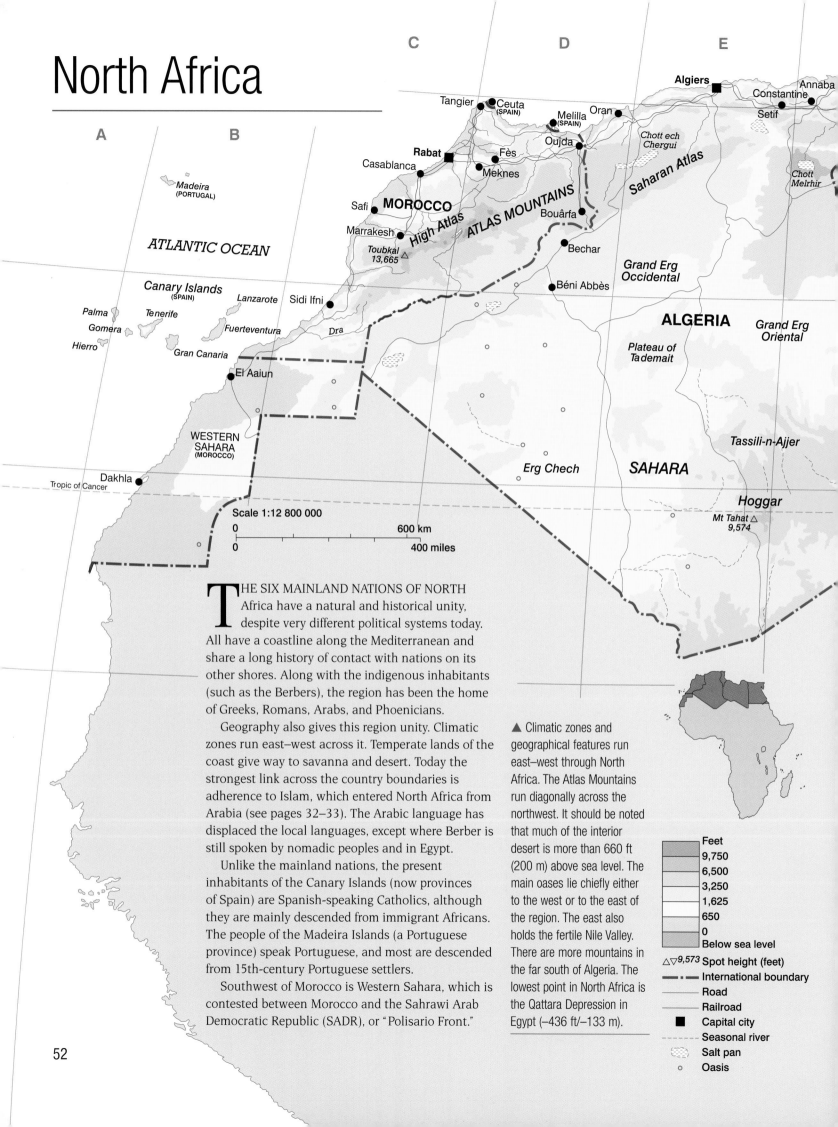

**A**      **B**      **C**      **D**      **E**

*Madeira*
(PORTUGAL)

Tangier   Ceuta (SPAIN)

Algiers   Annaba

Constantine

Oran

Setif

Melilla (SPAIN)

*Chott ech Chergui*

Oujda

**Rabat**

Casablanca   Fès

Meknes

*Saharan Atlas*

*Chott Melrhir*

Safi   **MOROCCO**

*ATLANTIC OCEAN*

*High Atlas*   **ATLAS MOUNTAINS**

Bouârfa

Marrakesh

*Toubkal* 13,665 △

Bechar

*Grand Erg Occidental*

*Canary Islands* (SPAIN)

Lanzarote

Sidi Ifni

Béni Abbès

**ALGERIA**

*Grand Erg Oriental*

*Palma*   *Tenerife*

*Gomera*   Fuerteventura

Dra

*Plateau of Tademait*

*Hierro*

*Gran Canaria*

El Aaiun

*Tassili-n-Ajjer*

**WESTERN SAHARA**
(MOROCCO)

*Erg Chech*   **SAHARA**

*Hoggar*

Dakhla

Tropic of Cancer

*Mt Tahat △ 9,574*

Scale 1:12 800 000

0        600 km

0        400 miles

T HE SIX MAINLAND NATIONS OF NORTH
Africa have a natural and historical unity,
despite very different political systems today.
All have a coastline along the Mediterranean and
share a long history of contact with nations on its
other shores. Along with the indigenous inhabitants
(such as the Berbers), the region has been the home
of Greeks, Romans, Arabs, and Phoenicians.

Geography also gives this region unity. Climatic
zones run east–west across it. Temperate lands of the
coast give way to savanna and desert. Today the
strongest link across the country boundaries is
adherence to Islam, which entered North Africa from
Arabia (see pages 32–33). The Arabic language has
displaced the local languages, except where Berber is
still spoken by nomadic peoples and in Egypt.

Unlike the mainland nations, the present
inhabitants of the Canary Islands (now provinces
of Spain) are Spanish-speaking Catholics, although
they are mainly descended from immigrant Africans.
The people of the Madeira Islands (a Portuguese
province) speak Portuguese, and most are descended
from 15th-century Portuguese settlers.

Southwest of Morocco is Western Sahara, which is
contested between Morocco and the Sahrawi Arab
Democratic Republic (SADR), or "Polisario Front."

▲ Climatic zones and
geographical features run
east–west through North
Africa. The Atlas Mountains
run diagonally across the
northwest. It should be noted
that much of the interior
desert is more than 660 ft
(200 m) above sea level. The
main oases lie chiefly either
to the west or to the east of
the region. The east also
holds the fertile Nile Valley.
There are more mountains in
the far south of Algeria. The
lowest point in North Africa is
the Qattara Depression in
Egypt (−436 ft/−133 m).

| Feet |
| --- |
| 9,750 |
| 6,500 |
| 3,250 |
| 1,625 |
| 650 |
| 0 |
| Below sea level |

△▽ 9,573 Spot height (feet)

▬ · ▬ International boundary

—— Road

—— Railroad

■ Capital city

- - - - Seasonal river

Salt pan

○ Oasis

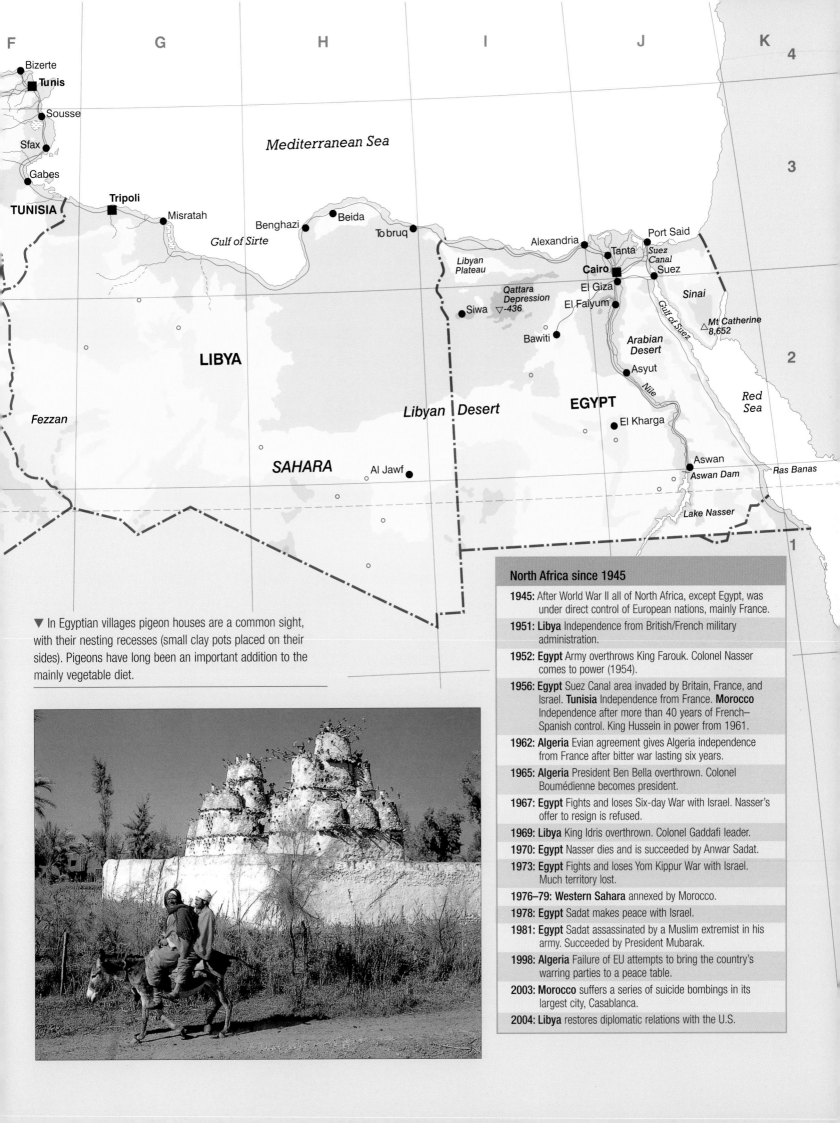

F    G    H    I    J    K    4

Bizerte
**Tunis**
Sousse
Sfax
Gabes
**TUNISIA**

**Tripoli**
Misratah
*Gulf of Sirte*
Benghazi
Beida
Tobruq

*Mediterranean Sea*

Alexandria
Tanta
Port Said
*Suez Canal*
**Cairo**
Suez
El Giza
*Sinai*
*Libyan Plateau*
*Qattara Depression* ▽-436
El Faiyum
Siwa
Bawiti
*Arabian Desert*
△ Mt Catherine 8,652

**LIBYA**

*Libyan  Desert*

Asyut

**EGYPT**

*Fezzan*

*Nile*

*Red Sea*

*Gulf of Suez*

**SAHARA**

Al Jawf

El Kharga

Aswan
Aswan Dam
Ras Banas

*Lake Nasser*

3

2

1

▼ In Egyptian villages pigeon houses are a common sight, with their nesting recesses (small clay pots placed on their sides). Pigeons have long been an important addition to the mainly vegetable diet.

### North Africa since 1945

**1945:** After World War II all of North Africa, except Egypt, was under direct control of European nations, mainly France.

**1951: Libya** Independence from British/French military administration.

**1952: Egypt** Army overthrows King Farouk. Colonel Nasser comes to power (1954).

**1956: Egypt** Suez Canal area invaded by Britain, France, and Israel. **Tunisia** Independence from France. **Morocco** Independence after more than 40 years of French–Spanish control. King Hussein in power from 1961.

**1962: Algeria** Evian agreement gives Algeria independence from France after bitter war lasting six years.

**1965: Algeria** President Ben Bella overthrown. Colonel Boumédienne becomes president.

**1967: Egypt** Fights and loses Six-day War with Israel. Nasser's offer to resign is refused.

**1969: Libya** King Idris overthrown. Colonel Gaddafi leader.

**1970: Egypt** Nasser dies and is succeeded by Anwar Sadat.

**1973: Egypt** Fights and loses Yom Kippur War with Israel. Much territory lost.

**1976–79: Western Sahara** annexed by Morocco.

**1978: Egypt** Sadat makes peace with Israel.

**1981: Egypt** Sadat assassinated by a Muslim extremist in his army. Succeeded by President Mubarak.

**1998: Algeria** Failure of EU attempts to bring the country's warring parties to a peace table.

**2003: Morocco** suffers a series of suicide bombings in its largest city, Casablanca.

**2004: Libya** restores diplomatic relations with the U.S.

# Nomadic Life

SOUTH OF THE FERTILE COASTAL STRIP WITH its good seasonal rains, much of North Africa is dry and barren desert, or semidesert, with scrub and grass suitable for pasture only part of the time. This is true also of other parts of the continent —the Horn of Africa, the Kalahari Desert in southern Africa, and the Sahel that stretches across West Africa. Except at oases or along riverbanks, very little can be grown in these desert areas.

## The desert peoples

For thousands of years most of the people who have lived in the world's desert areas have been shepherds and herdsmen, collectively known as "pastoralists." Because water and grass are scarce, they must move with their flocks and herds of sheep, cattle, and goats to find what they need, so are also called nomads (Latin *nomas*, meaning "wandering shepherd").

In some nations of Africa, such as Somalia and Chad, where drought is common, more than half of the population are still pastoral nomads. As time goes on and populations grow, their number will decrease because overgrazing causes erosion, which in turn causes the desert to spread. In addition, most governments prefer to govern settled populations and therefore encourage settlement.

## The Tuareg, nomads of Algeria

One of the best known nomadic peoples is the Tuareg. They are a Berber ethnic group originally from Libya and Algeria but now mostly concentrated in Niger and Mali. In southern Algeria, the Tuareg

move in large clan groups across the highland area known as the Hoggar. No one knows very much about their origins—the leading families are brown-skinned with sharp features. Their servants are generally darker-skinned Africans.

The Tuareg are Muslims, and with them, unusually, it is the men not the women who cover their faces with a veil. They live in tents made of leather stretched over a framework of poles. Camels carry the tents and all their goods when they move.

The Tuareg stay in one place as long as there is enough water and grass. They keep goats and sheep as well as camels, but the camels are the most important because camel milk is their chief food. In some areas where settled Africans grow wheat and sorghum, the Tuareg can buy or barter their produce.

▶ The Somali, another nomadic group, are found not only in Somalia but also in the north of Kenya, where they have been moving steadily for many years. Their way of life centers on waterholes.

▼ A nomadic family of Bedouin in Morocco sit at the door of their tent as a new day dawns. They keep sheep and goats rather than camels.

▶ The Kababis of northern Sudan are nomads who mostly use camels. Like almost all the northern nomads, they are Muslim. Women weave cloth strips that are sewn together to make the tent, and make patterned carpets to sit on. The tent has an outer room for the men and their visitors, and an inner room for the women and children.

# Cairo

ONE OF THE GREAT CITIES OF THE medieval and modern world, Cairo has a population in excess of 15 million, making it the largest city in Africa. It is not as old a city as one might expect in such an ancient country.

Cairo was founded in 642 C.E., when Muslim Arabs conquered Egypt. It replaced the ancient capital of Memphis, which lay 15 miles (24 km) to the south. Both cities are situated just above the flood level of the Nile River where it fans out into its enormous fertile delta.

## The history of Cairo

As with other great capital cities that began in early medieval times, Cairo's history is firmly linked to that of the whole country. From the time the Romans were overthrown in the seventh century, Egypt was ruled by a succession of Muslim dynasties. Cairo's greatest days were perhaps under the Fatimid dynasty (970–1171) and the great Saladin of Damascus and his family and Mamluk successors (1171–1516). From then until the Napoleonic invasion of 1798 its rulers were Ottoman Turks.

Modernization began in the 19th century, when first French and then British businessmen began involving themselves in the affairs of Egypt. Many Europeans came to live in the city, including professionals who introduced Western medicine and education. The city, which had been quite small at the time of the French invasion, began to expand markedly from the 1830s. Today, more than 15 percent of all Egyptians live there.

In 1856 the first railway (from Alexandria to Cairo) was completed, and from 1854 to 1869 the Suez Canal was built, funded by money from overseas. The ships passing through the new canal, together with high demand for Egyptian cotton during the American Civil War (1861–65), brought new prosperity to parts of Cairo.

Ismail Pasha, khedive (ruler) of Egypt from 1863 to 1879 encouraged the construction of a European-style city center that still forms Cairo's hub.

## Cairo's monuments

The enormous city, which is still growing, contains within itself the monuments of its long past, in its citadels, markets, tombs (including the Great Pyramid of Giza), and, above all, in its mosques and churches. The earliest mosque still remaining is that of Ahmed ibn Tulun, built 876–78. Cairo also has one of the oldest operating universities in the world, al-Azhar University, founded in 988 B.C.E.

Cairo, like the rest of Egypt, is mainly Muslim, but its ancient Christian church, originally a branch of the Eastern Orthodox Church, still exists. Its name, the Coptic Orthodox Church, preserves the old Roman word, *Aegyptus*. Its services are still held in "church Coptic." But in the rest of Africa, Egypt is known as Misri, from Misr, the original Arabic name of the settlement that became Cairo.

▶ A bazaar, a street of little shops and canopied stalls, located near the main mosque in Cairo. Sellers of food and clothes, craftsmen carrying on their work, porters making deliveries, all mingle with the crowds wanting to buy, bargain, or simply enjoy the noisy, colorful scene.

◀ The ancient al-Azhar University was founded as part of the al-Azhar mosque in 988 B.C.E. Like other large mosques, it became a *gami'a*, or Assembly Mosque, where theology was taught. It is now a normal university, but still trains Islamic theologians.

▶ Bowls, lamps, trays, and brass or copper cooking vessels are sold in the bazaar. Traditional homes have little furniture, and large metal trays placed on the floor or on a low stool are used at mealtimes as tables.

# West Africa

ALL EXCEPT THREE OF THE PRESENT NATIONS of West Africa were, from the mid-19th century to the mid-20th century, under French or British colonial rule. Liberia, although never a colony, has maintained close links with the United States; Guinea-Bissau and the islands that form Cape Verde were Portuguese colonies.

Before the colonial period the peoples of West Africa were organized in everything from small village communities to nations and empires. Some communities follow traditional religions. Islam is widespread, especially in the north, and there are many Christians as well. All these nations have sharp contrasts in geography and lifestyle between their fertile coast and inland semidesert regions.

### West Africa since 1945

**1945:** All of West Africa, except Liberia, under European colonial rule.

**1947: Nigeria** Kwame Nkrumah returns to the Gold Coast. Beginning of Convention Peoples Party, first modern African political party.

**1956: Nigeria** Discovery of oil in eastern Nigeria. **Senegal** Granted self-government by France.

**1957: Ghana** First black African state given independence by Britain.

**1958: Ghana** All African People's Conference meets in Accra. **Guinea** First French West African colony given independence.

**1960: Nigeria** Gains independence from Britain. **Mali-Senegal** Gains independence as short-lived Mali federation. **West Africa** All remaining French colonies gain independence.

**1961: Sierra Leone** Gains independence from Britain.

**1966: Nigeria** Parliamentary government overthrown by army, General Gowan becomes leader in second coup. **Ghana** Nkrumah overthrown—goes into exile.

**1967: Nigeria** Eastern region declares itself separate country—Biafra. Civil war begins.

**1970: Nigeria** End of civil war. Biafra starved into submission.

**1975: Nigeria** Gowan overthrown. Replaced by military-dominated government.

**1982: Ghana** Thousands of Ghanaian workers in Nigeria expelled from the country. **Senegal & Gambia** The two countries join together in a federation.

**1983: Upper Volta** Coup brings Thomas Sanham to power. The country's name is changed to Burkina Faso.

**2002: Sierra Leone** General election confirms the end of the country's 11-year civil war.

**2003: Liberia** President Charles Taylor resigns.

**2005: Liberia** Ellen Johnson-Sirleaf becomes first elected female president of an African country.

**2006: Liberia** Former President Charles Taylor extradited from Nigeria to face war crime charges before a U.N. tribunal.

▶ Most of West Africa lies less than 3,500 ft (1,100 m) above sea level. The highest point is Mt. Cameroon (13,354 ft/4,000 m), which is volcanic. The nations with a coast along the Gulf of Guinea have a fertile, once-forested strip backed by higher land, becoming semidesert in the north. The landlocked nations are largely desert and semidesert, except in their limited higher regions. The Niger River and its many tributaries are of great importance in the region's economy, as are the Niger and Volta River dams.

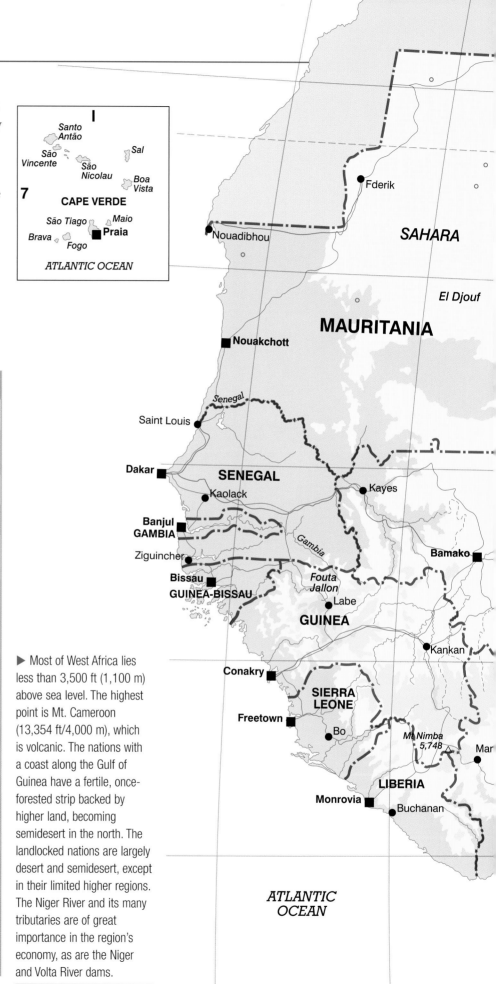

C    D    E    F    G    H

6

**Feet**
9,750
6,500
3,250
1,625
650
0

△13,354 Mountain peak (Feet)
━ ∙∙ ━ International boundary
━━━ Road
━━━ Railroad
■ Capital city
╌╌╌ Seasonal river
Marsh
○ Oasis

Tropic of Cancer

5

*SAHARA*

*Djado Plateau*

*Adrar des Iforas*

*Air*

**MALI**

**NIGER**

4

Timbuktu   *Niger*

Gao

● Agades

*Grand Erg de Bilma*

Mopti

*Bandiagara Plateau*

*Sahel*

*Sahel*

Zinder

*Lake Chad*

3

Segou

Ouahigouya

■ **Niamey**

Sokoto

Katsina

Nguru

**BURKINA FASO**

■ **Ouagadougou**

Kano

Maiduguri

Sikasso

Bobo Dioulasso

Zaria

Maroua

Kaduna

*Jos Plateau*

Garoua

**BENIN**

*Kainji Reservoir*

*Comoe*

*Black Volta*

Tamale

Parakou

*Kainji Dam*

**NIGERIA**

■ **Abuja**

*Benue*

Ngaoundéré

2

*Buí Dam*

Sokode

Ilorin

Ogbomosho

Oshogbo

*Adamawa Highlands*

**CÔTE D'IVOIRE**

**GHANA**

*Lake Volta*

**TOGO**

Ibadan

Ife

Bouaké

Abeokuta

*Niger*

Enugu

**CAMEROON**

■ **Yamoussoukro**

**Porto Novo**

Lagos

Benin City

Onitsha

loa

Kumasi

*Akosombo Dam*

*Volta*

■ **Lomé**

Cotonou

Igbo-Ukwe

Nkongsamba

Abidjan

■ **Accra**

Port Harcourt

*Sanaga*

Douala

Sekondi Takoradi

*Mt Cameroon* △ 13,354

■ **Yaoundé**

1

*Bight of Benin*

*Gulf of Guinea*

Scale 1:11 000 000

0 ────────── 600 km

0 ────────── 400 miles

59

# A Dogon Village

THE DOGON PEOPLE ARE FARMERS WHO live in the east of southern Mali near its border with Burkina Faso. Their home is the dry and rocky Bandiagara Plateau, within the curve of the Niger. Not far north are the deserts where nomads make a difficult living. The Dogon have apparently lived on the Bandiagara Plateau for some 500 years. They are descendants of the Tellem people, with whom they share a similar material culture.

The plateau where the Dogon live is edged with very steep cliffs and is covered with rocky debris. Some Dogon live on the plateau. Others live at the foot of the cliffs and even on the cliffs themselves. Fertile land is precious, so every scrap is used.

## Cliff-face dwellings

The houses, tightly grouped into family compounds, cluster together in large villages. Between the small square mud-built houses are tall towerlike granaries, or food stores, with thatched roofs. Houses and storehouses are joined with mud walls to form the compound (see also pages 46–47).

Their traditional religion is very important to the Dogon. In every village there is a *hogon*, a priest who leads the ceremonies and also passes on the old stories of his peoples, such as how God made the world. The very way in which a Dogon courtyard is arranged, its furnishings, and even the position of the fireplace and entrance door and walls, serve to link the present with the past and to remind the family of these stories.

## Crops and farming

Despite the difficulties of their terrain, the Dogon grow enough grain for themselves and some left over for sale or barter. Millet is important in religious ceremonies (offerings are made at planting and harvest times).

Sorghum and other kinds of grain are grown. So are vegetables and—where there is enough land—rice. The Dogon's plateau is not as dry as the surrounding area, and rain gets trapped in pools in the rocks. Terraces are made to grow crops on, and weeds are composted to make the most of the soil.

The men like to hunt, but that produces little food. Like some of their nearer neighbors, the Dogon fish or keep stock—some cattle and donkeys, but mainly sheep, goats, and hens.

▶ Most daily activity in a Dogon village is in the open—houses are dark and small. Here, a man weaves cotton cloth, used especially for the clothes of the older men. Dyed blue with indigo, it is made into tunics and wide pantaloons. The compound elder (far right) looks on. Dogon men almost always wear bonnets. They decorate their clothing and sandals with cowrie shells. Women wearing skirts of shop-bought cloth carry baskets of grain.

◀ A Dogon village seen from a cave in the cliff face. The flat-roofed mud houses with taller round granaries and food stores cluster together in family compounds, separated by narrow alleys. The plain beyond, once well wooded, is now treeless.

# Yoruba Religion

THE MAJORITY OF YORUBA PEOPLE IN Nigeria, Benin, and Togo are now Christians or Muslims, but their traditional religion has not completely disappeared. Also, because many of the slaves who were taken to the West Indies and Brazil were Yoruba, some of their old religious practices continue on the other side of the Atlantic.

## The Yoruba hierarchy of gods

The Yoruba's political system was based on a kingdom, with chiefs and a nobility, but was not very unified. Their religion, though sharing features of other African religions (see pages 34–35), was diverse with four ranks of gods or spiritual beings. They numbered about 400 in all, with different places having favorite gods.

The Supreme Being is called Olorun (also Olodumare, "owner of heaven"), who holds the ultimate unity at the top. Ranked beneath him are subordinate gods and goddesses, known as *orisha*. Obatala, the god of creation, is the most important of these gods.

In the third rank are the spirits of great ancestors, humans who have become gods. There is Shango, god of thunder, and—most effective and widely found—Ogun, god of iron and war. Then there are the spirits connected with the earth (*Ile*), and those associated with rivers, mountains, and trees.

Olorun, the Supreme Being, is seen as immortal, all-knowing, all-powerful, and totally just. Prayers are made to him, but there are no shrines in his honor. It is thought that the subordinate gods and the other spiritual beings who have shrines dedicated to them will pass on any offerings. Many rituals end with the words: "May Olorun accept it."

From the outside a shrine may look like an ordinary Yoruba house, but it contains carvings representing the gods to whom it is dedicated. Inside, priests wait for those who bring offerings to the gods or come to consult.

## Prayer, worship, and masquerades

Men and women pray to the gods in private and they also join with others to worship them. The Yoruba, like most African peoples, respect ancestors and make sacrifices to them. Dogs, for example, are sacrificed to Ogun.

The Yoruba have highly developed forms of "divination" (finding out about future events). When they are puzzled about which course of action to follow they will ask a priest, some of whom act as

▲ Masked dancers perform a masquerade known as Egungun, a celebration in which the spirit of a dead person "visits." Their masks often depict animal heads, and their clothes are always richly decorated.

▲ Nature spirits may be male or female. Not all are good: Oya, goddess of the Niger, brings strong gales. Yemoja (above) is good: she is the goddess of water, rivers, and streams and is seen as the source of all life-giving water.

▲ Shango, the powerful god of thunder, was once a fierce Oyo king. Gifts are made to him so that he will not destroy houses and men. Shrines to Shango are also found in North and South America and the West Indies.

diviners. To find out what the future holds, the priest may, for example, consult the way palm nuts lie on a special tray. The Yoruba may also consult an "oracle," by questioning a god or spirit at a shrine, again through a priest or diviner. There was an especially famous one at Ife, the religious heart of Yorubaland. Special objects in the Yoruba system of divination include a bell, made of wood or ivory, used to summon the oracular spirit, and lots, which may be core shells or animal teeth.

Part of Yoruba worship takes the form of special dances, some of them masquerades, or masked dances, that bring the people together to honor the gods and spirits. Most of the dances are important in showing respect to the dead and keeping health and harmony among the living.

One famous masquerade is *egungun*, in which an ancestor's spirit returns to the community to visit his "children." Dancers are clothed in materials that are whirled about in changing forms, making the ancestors "manifest," or appear. Every single part of the dancer's body must be hidden, otherwise the spell will be broken.

Another dance, *gelede*, danced in western Yorubaland, is performed to entertain and please the malign (bad) spirits or witches so that they will not harm the community.

▲ Carved figures of Eshu, the trickster god. A messenger between gods and men, he can do good and evil. No traditional believer fails to make gifts to him. One of these figures is male and one female, showing the different forms in which Eshu appears.

▶ Some gods are local; others, such as Ogun, are known throughout Yorubaland. Sacrifices to Ogun are made everywhere. He helps hunters, blacksmiths, butchers, and barbers and, nowadays, truck and taxi drivers. It is by Ogun that traditional believers take an oath in court.

◀ In Yorubaland priests are attached to temples and shrines erected in honor of the subordinate gods, ancestor gods, and the nature spirits, whose images are kept in the shrines. After training, the priests are seen as competent to offer the sacrifices, usually goats or chickens.

# Asante Ceremonial Regalia

THE KINGDOM OF ASANTE IN THE MODERN state of Ghana became powerful in the late 17th century. At that time, the chief of the town of Kumasi, Osei Tutu, declared himself ruler (or Asantehene) of the Asante people. Together with Okomfo Anokye, his chief priest, Osei Tutu won the allegiance of other Asante chiefs, altered the constitution (the laws by which a country is governed), and made changes to the ceremonial regalia, particularly the royal stool.

In Asante, as elsewhere in West Africa, the king was generally regarded as the link, or intermediary, between heaven and earth. Up until Osei Tutu's time,

▶ Chiefs with their wives and attendants await the Asantehene. A musician plays a side-blown horn.

▼ Chiefs holding gold-plated state swords and protected by umbrellas attend the funeral of Asantehene Sir Agyeman Prempeh II (1970). In the late 1930s he did much to restore the glories of the old ceremonies.

▲ Chiefs wearing their ceremonial gold-plated headdresses. Their robes are worn thrown over one shoulder.

▼ Musicians playing side-blown ivory horns at an Asante state ceremony. Each chief has his own horn-blower who sounds an individual note. This note identifies the chief and tells his people of his arrival. Each horn has its own name. Drums and gongs are also used in the ceremonies.

the royal throne (a stool) had symbolized the individual ruler. Osei Tutu substituted it with a special Golden Stool, which he said had descended from heaven into his lap, symbolizing the Asante nation. Thus, even when the ruler died, the nation would live on in the stool.

### The Odwira Festival

Every year the people of Asante assembled after the yam harvest for a national festival, the Odwira. This festival was to honor the nation, and so remind the people of their unity with their kingdom and also their unity with their spirit ancestors. Cleansing rituals, called "purificatory ceremonies," linked the living and the dead.

The Golden Stool was hung with the golden death masks of enemy generals who had been defeated by Asante armies. During the festival it was carried in procession and placed on a throne, without ever touching the ground.

The royal power was also shown in the regalia—clothes, ornaments, and decorations—worn or carried by the Asantehene and his chiefs. Vast umbrellas topped by golden ornaments shielded them from the sun, and they wore gold rings and headdresses, and carried gold-plated swords. Since Asante lies in a gold-bearing region and gold has been important for the kingdom's trade, the Odwira Festival with its very visible use of gold gave a sense of wealth, dignity, pride, and—above all—unity throughout the various Asante groups.

### The British assume control

As Britain extended its power in West Africa, there were clashes with the Asante, and the area became a British protectorate in 1896. Britain wanted more control over the West African coast in order to protect its valuable trade.

As early as 1874 the capital of the Asante kingdom, Kumasi, had been sacked. Later the king, Prempeh, was removed, and by 1901 the area was annexed with the southern area of what is now Ghana as the colony of the Gold Coast.

The British administrators, knowing but not understanding the power of the Golden Stool, continued to use it, often in ways that distressed the people of Asante.

In 1935 the Golden Stool was given back to the Asante people and a new Asantehene, Prempeh II, revived the ceremonies. Thus the Asante were once more united, at least in a symbolic way.

# Nigerian Art: Bronze- and Brass-casting

THROUGHOUT NIGERIA THERE HAS BEEN A long tradition of producing bronze and brass statues, masks, and ornaments. There seem to have been many centers of production.

At Benin a highly developed culture flourished in the 16th and 17th centuries, before the slave trade caused a long decline. As well as brass-casting, the Benin arts of fine ivory carving and woodcarving are renowned. When the palace of Benin was looted by the British in 1897, large numbers of high quality brass sculptures were taken (most are now in British and German museums). A British official described what was stolen as "a regular harvest of loot!"

## An incomplete history

From the 1920s quantities of metal objects were found in southeastern Nigeria, often at places where there was no tradition of metalwork. The history of Nigerian bronze-casting is far from complete, but recent work at Igbo Ukwu in south central Nigeria suggests it began before the ninth century C.E.

Most of the extremely large number of metal objects known have been found accidentally—for example, the hoard excavated by Thurston Shaw at Igbo Ukwu in 1937 or, in the same year, the "Ife bronzes" (actually brass), which were found near the palace of Ife. They are surely only a small part of what must have existed.

▲ This fine figure of a dwarf is one of the most lifelike found at Benin. It belongs to the earliest period (16th century) and is close in style to the Ife tradition. Ife is thought to have been the original home of the technique of bronze-casting.

◀ A plaque from the palace at Benin City. A 17th-century Dutch traveler described the palace as having "wooden pillars encased in copper, where their victories are depicted." This plaque from such a pillar shows hunters and leopards against a background of leaves.

▶ Also from Benin is this superb brass ram's head. It probably dates from the 17th century and was an ornament on a belt worn by a chief. Most "bronzes" from Benin seem to have been for ceremonial use or for the ornamentation of the leading people.

### Methods of bronze-casting

Bronze is an alloy of copper and tin—if zinc is used with the copper, brass is the result. If lead is added, the alloy is more easily worked. Lead, tin, and zinc are all found in Nigeria; copper was imported, perhaps from Niger.

Most Nigerian bronzes were produced by a process known as the lost wax method. A clay core (an exact model of the final object) was covered with a layer of wax and then with a layer of clay, making a kind of sandwich. The result, the cast, was held in place with iron pins and sun-dried. The wax or latex was then melted out through holes left in the outer clay covering and replaced by molten bronze or brass. When the metal had hardened, the outer clay was removed to reveal the bronze or brass sculpture.

### Brass-casting at Benin and Ife

Benin City was by the 15th century the center of a powerful state in the forest area west of the Niger Delta. To the present day there has been a continuous history of brass-casting. At Benin the industry seems to have been at its height from the 16th to the 19th centuries.

Northwest of Benin, at Ife, the exquisitely fine, naturalistic brass heads date back as far as the 12th century. These probably also relate to Nok terra-cotta (earthenware) sculptures which go back another 1,000 years. Although all of the Benin and Ife sculptures are, in fact, made of brass, they have traditionally been called the Ife and Benin Bronzes.

An amazing number of skills must have existed among local peoples for such bronzes to be produced. First the modeler or sculptor has to produce the clay and wax core. Then, when the metal object is broken out of its clay case, it has to be filed down, smoothed, and finished.

When we add to this the transportation and production of the ores, it is clear that such work would only be produced in a prosperous and stable society, usually with a king or chief who was the sponsor, or patron, of the industry.

◀ One of a group of bronzes from the lower Niger. Full of lifelike detail, it shows a hunter returning home with an antelope slung over his shoulders, its legs tied.

▼ A horse and rider with elaborate headdress, in the rather stiff, court style of the mid-17th century. Brass-casting in Benin was under the direction of its Oba (ruler).

# W. Central Africa

**A**LL THE NATIONS OF WEST CENTRAL AFRICA were at some time colonies of France, Spain, Belgium, or Portugal. There is an immense geographical range, from the tropical rainforests of the Democratic Republic of the Congo and Gabon through grasslands to the desert of northern Chad. Ways of life are as varied as the landscapes.

## Different peoples and cultures

In the northern deserts of landlocked Chad are nomadic pastoral peoples, such as the Fulani, who are Arabic-speaking Muslims. Most people, however, follow traditional religions, and some are Christians. The people outside the desert areas mainly combine agriculture with keeping stock or, especially in the Democratic Republic of the Congo, with fishing.

The Mbuti, and other people of small stature, are hunter-gatherers living in the forests (see pages

70–71). They were in the region long before the majority population of Negroid agriculturalists, Bantu-speaking peoples, who probably arrived in the second millennium. Their own language has long since disappeared and they share local languages and exchange goods with these farming peoples.

It is believed that the Bantu-speaking peoples spread out from these forests, eventually migrating into East and southern Africa. South of the Central African Republic most people speak Bantu

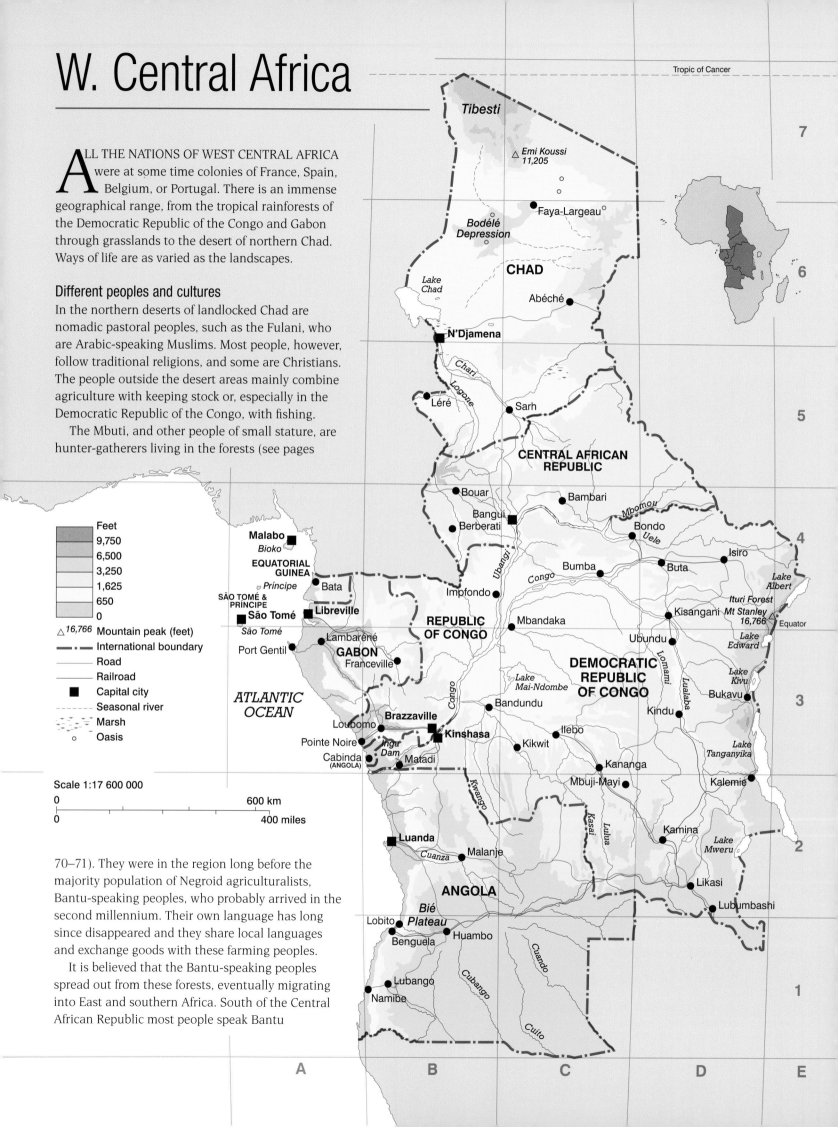

Feet
9,750
6,500
3,250
1,625
650
0

△16,766 Mountain peak (feet)
▪—·— International boundary
Road
Railroad
■ Capital city
--------- Seasonal river
Marsh
○ Oasis

Scale 1:17 600 000

0 ——————————— 600 km

0 ——————————— 400 miles

Tibesti

△ Emi Koussi 11,205

Faya-Largeau

Bodélé Depression

CHAD

Lake Chad

Abéché

■ N'Djamena

Chari

Logone

Léré

Sarh

CENTRAL AFRICAN REPUBLIC

Bouar

Bambari

Bangui

Berberati

Mbomou

Bondo

Uele

Isiro

Ubangi

Bumba

Congo

Buta

Lake Albert

Malabo ■
Bioko

EQUATORIAL GUINEA

○ Príncipe

Bata

Impfondo

SÃO TOMÉ & PRÍNCIPE

■ São Tomé

São Tomé

Libreville

REPUBLIC OF CONGO

Mbandaka

Ituri Forest

Kisangani  Mt Stanley 16,766

Ubundu

Equator

Lake Edward

Lambaréné

Port Gentil

GABON

Franceville

Congo

Lake Mai-Ndombe

DEMOCRATIC REPUBLIC OF CONGO

Lomami

Lualaba

Lake Kivu

ATLANTIC OCEAN

Bandundu

Bukavu

Loubomo

Brazzaville

■ Kinshasa

Ilebo

Kindu

Pointe Noire

Inga Dam

Matadi

Kikwit

Lake Tanganyika

Cabinda (ANGOLA)

Kananga

Mbuji-Mayi

Kalemie

Kwango

Kasai

Lulua

Kamina

Lake Mweru

Luanda ■

Cuanza

Malanje

ANGOLA

Likasi

Bié Plateau

Lobito

Huambo

Benguela

Cuando

Lubumbashi

Lubango

Namibe

Cubango

Cuito

► A manganese mine at Moanda near Franceville in southeastern Gabon. Minerals such as manganese and uranium are bringing prosperity and change to Gabon, the Republic of Congo, and other countries of west central Africa. Gold, diamonds, and iron ore are exported from nations in this region. The south of the Democratic Republic of the Congo has great mineral resources, but recently this wealth has contributed to the country's civil war.

► Fulani (Fulbe) people are found across West Africa from the Atlantic to southwest Chad. They do not speak Bantu but Nigritic. Many are Muslim. They vary greatly in appearance and in their way of life; a large number are nomadic.

◄ In southern Chad near Léré, the main agricultural region of the country, villagers store their grain (mainly millet) in tall granaries made of clay and designed to keep out pests such as rats.

◄ There is great geographic diversity in this region, which stretches from the Tropic of Cancer across the equator to 18°S. The area covers the desert of inland Chad, the plains and high plateau of Angola (where cattle can be raised), and the vast plateau of wooded savanna and the forested river valleys of the Democratic Republic of the Congo. The rivers are a means of communication and an important food source.

languages. (French and Portuguese are the most widely-spoken second languages.)

Political organization in this region before modern times varied from the tiny bands of the Mbuti to chiefdoms or kingdoms such as Kongo, Loango, and Ndongo. Large village settlements, or small towns, with the houses laid out in regular rows, are common—in contrast to the rather less regular groupings found in North or East African villages.

Cotton, coffee, rice, rubber, and oil palms are all grown. Several of the nations have oil reserves, and the Democratic Republic of the Congo is especially rich in minerals. In the extreme southeast, on its border with Zambia, it forms a part of the Copper Belt (see pages 84–85), and it exports other minerals (tin, gold, manganese) and also diamonds.

Since independence there has been a good deal of political instability in all these nations except the three smallest states—Gabon and Republic of Congo (both formerly part of French Equatorial Africa), and Equatorial Guinea (formerly Spanish Guinea). Angola, which was poorly developed by Portugal, only achieved a shaky independence in 1975.

| West central Africa since 1944 |
|---|
| **1944–45:** Brazzaville (**French Congo**) Conference maps out future for French colonies in area. |
| **1960:** Chad, Central African Republic, Gabon, Republic of Congo (formerly French Congo), **Belgian Congo** Become independent. **Belgian Congo** Descends into civil war as Katanga, its richest region, secedes. |
| **1965:** **Belgian Congo** General Mobutu overthrows civilian government. **Central African Republic** Colonel Bokassa comes to power and later begins reign of terror. |
| **1968:** **Equatorial Guinea** Gains independence from Spain. |
| **1971:** **Belgian Congo** Changes name to Zaïre. |
| **1975:** **Angola** Becomes independent from Portugal but civil war breaks out. |
| **1983:** **Chad** French soldiers sent to Chad to fight against Libyan-backed rebels. |
| **1996:** **Chad** Peace terms agreed and new multiparty constitution created. |
| **1997:** **Zaïre** Mobuto flees after rebellion. Country is renamed Democratic Republic of the Congo by President Laurent-Désiré Kabila. |
| **2001:** **Democratic Republic of the Congo** President Kabila assassinated. |
| **2002:** **Angola** Africa's longest-running civil war ends. |
| **2003:** **Democratic Republic of the Congo** Transitional government established after Pretoria Accord signed, but fighting continues. |

# A Mbuti Encampment

LEGENDS ALL OVER THE WORLD MENTION "little people." In parts of Africa live people who are smaller than their neighbors and who follow a different way of life. In Kenya and Tanzania the Dorobo and Kindiga peoples living among the Maasai are hunters and not cattle keepers. They tend to be smaller than all their neighbors and speak a different language.

In the tropical rainforests of the Democratic Republic of the Congo are people of short stature. Europeans once gave them the name pygmies, from the Greek word meaning "undersized." There are a number of groups of such people who live by hunting and by gathering forest plants and fruit. Their origins are unknown but genetic studies suggest that, like the San of southern Africa (see pages 88–89), they are descended from some of the most ancient people on Earth.

## Mbuti of the Ituri Forest

We know most about the Mbuti of the Ituri Forest in the Democratic Republic of the Congo. Adult men average less than 5 feet (1.5 m) tall. They are slightly built, light brown in skin color, but otherwise not very different from their taller neighbors. They have no chiefs, but live in family groups joined in small bands, and move often to hunt and gather food. For huts or shelters they build dome-shaped frameworks

▼ A clearing in the rainforest, in which a band of Mbuti has set up an encampment. A man prepares for a hunt armed with bow, arrows, and net, while a woman returns with fruit. Traditional bark cloth is being prepared by beating bark with a stone mallet, and a mother adorns her child with dye.

▲ In the clearing around their shelters, a band of Mbuti performs a ceremonial dance. Here, their clothing is made from bunches of leaves. The Mbuti live in the far north of the Democratic Republic of the Congo.

of saplings covered with leaves. Their clothing was traditionally made from skins or from bark cloth. The men hunt with spears, and bows and arrows, and also trap small game in nets made of twine.

The Ituri Forest Mbuti believe in a "high god," a kind god of the forest to whom they pray and make sacrifices. They believe that they please their god by living in harmony with the forest. Although they once had their own language, it is now lost. All the Mbuti groups now speak the Bantu language of their farming neighbors, and they obtain goods that they need from these people. Grain and vegetables are not readily available to the Mbuti, so they obtain them in exchange for meat, bone, and ivory.

# Northeast Africa

THIS REGION IS SOMETIMES KNOWN AS THE "Horn of Africa." Its people in Djibouti, Somalia, and eastern Ethiopia are Muslims, and mostly live as nomadic herders struggling against a harsh climate. Although the nomadic tribes are often at war, they have much in common in their culture and way of life. Sudan and the rest of Ethiopia present great contrasts within themselves and with the eastern region.

Sudan is very much a bridge between the lighter-skinned peoples of Islamic Africa to the north and the darker-skinned non-Muslim people in its own southern area (although here many of those who once followed traditional religions are now either Christian or Muslim).

Ethiopia is an exception to almost all general statements about Africa. Within its mountainous highlands live peoples who have for centuries been Christians, Jews, or Muslims. Here too are found followers of traditional religions and others who only recently converted to Christianity.

Britain and France were the main colonial powers in Sudan, Somalia, and Djibouti. Italy ruled part of Somalia and (from 1936 to 1941) Ethiopia, which had kept its independence for centuries.

▶ Stretching inland from the Horn of Africa and the Red Sea, this is a region of contrasts. Most of Sudan and almost the whole of Somalia is low, hot and dry, while Ethiopia is largely high plateau with highlands of 6,600 ft (2,000 m) and many peaks more than 13,000 ft (4,000 m) high. In the south of Sudan along the White Nile are the huge Sudd swamps, where masses of vegetation restrict river transportation. The White Nile originating in Uganda and the Blue Nile from Ethiopia meet at the capital city of Sudan, Khartoum.

## Northeast Africa since 1945

**1945: Somalia** South Somaliland returned to Italy by Britain.

**1952: Ethiopia** Eritrea (former Italian colony) joined to Ethiopia by United Nations.

**1956: Sudan** Gains independence from Britain. Civil war between Christian South and Muslim North until 1972.

**1960: Somalia** Italian and British Somalilands join together as one independent country.

**1963: Ethiopia** In Addis Ababa the Organization of African Unity (OAU) is formed at a meeting of all independent African states.

**1969: Somalia** General Siad Barre becomes head of state.

**1974: Ethiopia** Emperor Haile Selassie overthrown. Empire abolished.

**1975: Ethiopia** Colonel Mengistu comes to power. Allies Ethiopia to USSR. Rebellion in Eritrea gathers force.

**1977: Djibouti** Gains independence from France.

**1983: Ethiopia** Drought and war with Eritrea causes one of worst famines ever known. Millions die in spite of massive food and medical aid from Europe and America.

**1993: Eritrea** Independence of Eritrea recognized.

**2003: Sudan** Major violence erupts between government-supported Arab Janjaweed militias and non-Arab rebel groups in the Darfur region.

**2006: Sudan** Death toll from the Darfur conflict estimated at between 70,000 and 400,000, with around 2 million people displaced.

A     B

Darfur
Jabal Marrah △ 10,131
Nyala ●
El Fasher ●
En Nahud ●
**SUDAN**
Lol
Wau ●

◀ The Shilluk people of southern Sudan choose a *reth* (king), who represents their divine hero-god Nyikang. Here, at the coronation of a new *reth*, an effigy of Nyikang, made of ostrich feathers, is carried on a 10-day procession to the town of Fashoda.

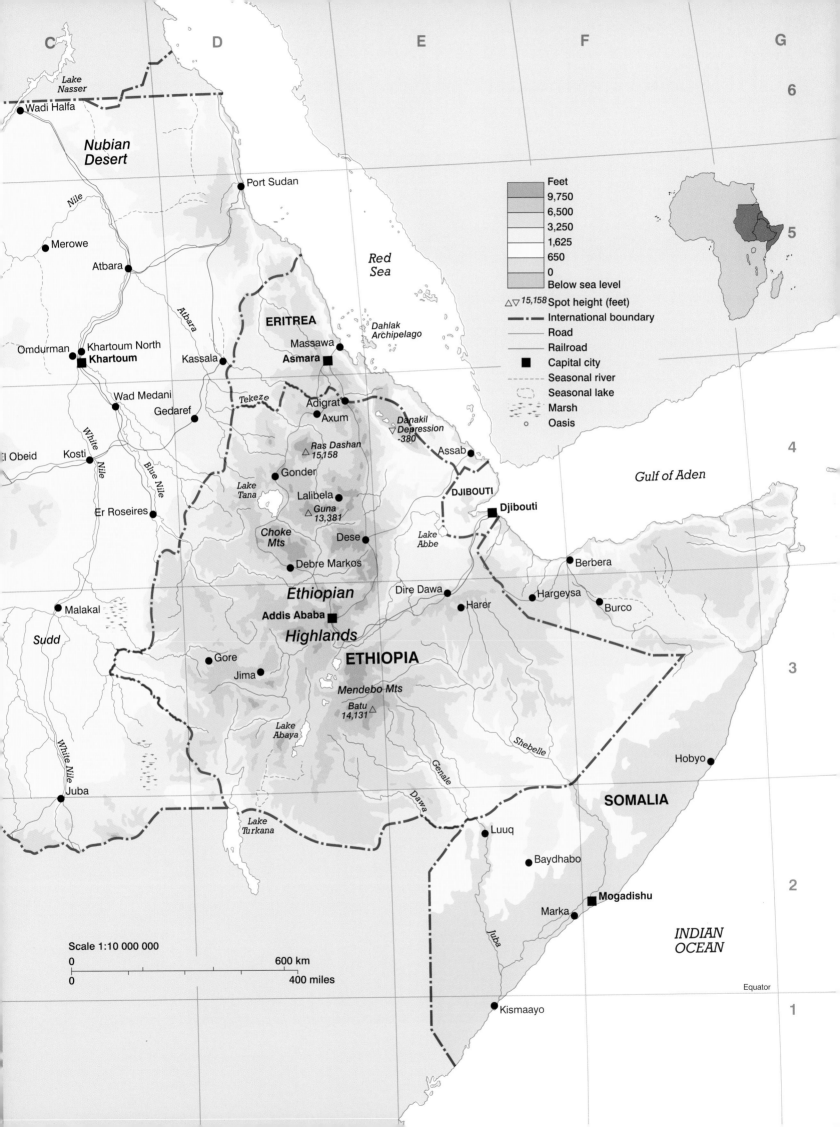

C　　　　　　　　　D　　　　　　　E　　　　　　　　F　　　　　G

6

*Lake Nasser*

• Wadi Halfa

*Nubian Desert*

*Nile*

• Port Sudan

• Merowe

Atbara •

*Atbara*

Omdurman •　Khartoum North •
　　　　　　■ **Khartoum**

Kassala •

**ERITREA**

Massawa •
**Asmara** ■

*Red Sea*

▽ *Dahlak Archipelago*

5

Feet
9,750
6,500
3,250
1,625
650
0
Below sea level

△▽ *15,158* Spot height (feet)
—··— International boundary
—— Road
—— Railroad
■ Capital city
- - - Seasonal river
Seasonal lake
Marsh
○ Oasis

Wad Medani •
Gedaref •

El Obeid •
Kosti •

*White Nile*

*Blue Nile*

Er Roseires •

Adigrat •
Axum •

*Tekeze*

*Ras Dashan*
*15,158* △

Gonder •

*Lake Tana*

Lalibela •
*Guna*
*13,381* △

*Danakil Depression*
▽ *-380*

Assab •

**DJIBOUTI**

■ **Djibouti**

*Gulf of Aden*

4

*Choke Mts*

Dese •

Debre Markos •

*Ethiopian*

*Lake Abbe*

Berbera •

Malakal •

*Sudd*

Dire Dawa •

Hargeysa •

Burco •

**Addis Ababa** ■

Harer •

*Highlands*

Gore •

**ETHIOPIA**

Jima •

*Mendebo Mts*

*Batu*
*14,131* △

*Lake Abaya*

*Shebelle*

Hobyo •

3

*White Nile*

Juba •

*Genale*

**SOMALIA**

*Lake Turkana*

*Dawa*

Luuq •

Baydhabo •

2

*Juba*

Marka •
**Mogadishu** ■

*INDIAN OCEAN*

Scale 1:10 000 000

0 ———————— 600 km
0 ———————— 400 miles

Equator

• Kismaayo

1

# Christians in Ethiopia

THERE HAVE BEEN CHRISTIANS LIVING IN parts of what is now Ethiopia (the old kingdom of Axum) since the fourth century C.E., which was when Christianity became the state religion—although it was probably only a minority religion until the 12th century. It was the most southern of a series of Christian countries that stretched south along the Nile.

From the ninth century, as with nearly all the other Christian kingdoms of North Africa and the Nile, the Ethiopian Church came under threat from Islam. However, the mountainous terrain that has always kept much of Ethiopia isolated allowed it to survive, albeit in a weakened form.

Relations were kept up with the Ethiopian Church's nearest Christian neighbor, the Coptic Church of Egypt, although the two differed in teaching. In fact, until 1951 the archbishop of the Ethiopian Orthodox Church was always an Egyptian, appointed by the Orthodox patriarch of Alexandria. Today, about 40 percent of Ethiopia's population are Christians.

## The administration of the Church

The Ethiopian Church retains many features of other eastern churches, such as a dual clergy of priests and monks. The Ethiopian Church is led by an archbishop

(the Abuna) and bishops (churches of this kind are called "episcopal"). Under them are priests and deacons (*dabtara*). Some priests marry; others remain unmarried and are monks. Before a man becomes a priest, he must be a *dabtara* for a while, Some *dabtara* never become priests, but work for the church as musicians, teachers, and clerks. It is the priests who lead the worship and who take services for baptism, holy communion, marriages, and funerals.

Only the unmarried priests can become bishops. In their services the priests use the old Semitic language, Ge'ez, from which the Amharic language, which is now used every day, descended.

◄ Education for the service of the church, including the reading of Ge'ez, usually takes place in monastery schools. Here a young deacon learns from older clergy in a monastery in Axum, Tigre. In the Ethiopian Church it is common for the deacons to be better educated than the more senior clergy.

▼ An Ethiopian priest, in his ceremonial robes, holds two of the hand crosses that are carried in procession. Crosses of every kind are a special feature of the Ethiopian Church—they are worn around the neck, carried, painted, and embroidered. Some Christians even have a cross tattooed on their wrist or forehead, a sign that cannot be removed.

◄ The cross shape of St. George's Church and the three crosses carved on its roof show clearly. These rock churches are built by digging a deep trench and excavating within the block. The trench round this 13th-century church is about 40 ft (12 m) deep.

◀ St. George (Beta Giyorgis) at Lalibela. The church rises 36 ft (11 m) from the rock base out of which it is hewn.

▶ In many Ethiopian churches are murals telling stories from the Bible or from the lives of saints. Here St. George, killing the dragon, is shown with a group of Ethiopian cherubs (at Lake Tana, to the west of Lalibela).

▲ A rock-cut path to one of the churches at Lalibela, itself carved out of the rock face. The pinkish color of the soft tufa rock can be seen. The largest of the rock churches is Beta Madhane 'Alem, "House of the Redeemer of the World." It is 110 ft (33 m) long and 38 ft (11 m) high.

## Teachings and festivals

In most respects the teachings of the Ethiopian Church are very close to those of the other Oriental Orthodox and Eastern Orthodox churches, and especially to the Coptic Orthodox Church of Egypt. But it has kept some customs similar to those of Judaism, and some that probably continue parts of the old pre-Christian traditional religions. These include the keeping of the Sabbath (Saturday) as well as Sunday, circumcision for all males, laws about purification and cleanliness, and animal sacrifices.

The Ark of the Covenant is given an important place in every church. Apart from services held on the Sabbath and Sundays, special festivals such as Christmas and Easter are kept. One great festival is that of the Baptism, in which the people go in procession to a lake or river. The priest blesses the water and the people bathe in the water, so recalling their own baptism.

At the festivals the *dabtara* play musical instruments (harps, rattles, and drums), and each priest beats the rhythm with a special baton called a prayer stick.

## The great stone churches

In the 12th century King Gadla Lalibela began to build wonderful churches at a place that is now called Lalibela. It is a remote mountain village in Welo Province, north of Addis Ababa, but it was once the capital of Ethiopia. King Gadla Lalibela may have begun his church-building to make his rule acceptable and certainly to enhance his city.

The churches were cut out of a soft volcanic rock called tufa, which hardens after cutting. Full of paintings and carvings, they are a wonderful exhibition of a church that has continued for 16 centuries despite every possible kind of difficulty.

# East Africa

BEFORE WORLD WAR I EAST AFRICA WAS under either British or German colonial rule. After the war the area known as German East Africa became Tanganyika, a British colony. The two small kingdoms of Rwanda and Burundi became Belgian colonies. Uganda, Kenya, and Zanzibar continued under British rule. Since World War II all these countries have become independent.

In the north and northeast of Uganda and Kenya, along the coasts and in some parts of Tanzania, Islam is strong. Inland, most regions have large Christian communities, with others following their traditional beliefs.

Languages of several families (such as Luo, Luyia, and Nandi) are found next to each other along the equator. The majority of the people speak Bantu languages, but in the north of Uganda and down the Great Rift Valley in Kenya and Tanzania people speak Nilo-Saharan languages. In Kenya's northeast are nomadic Somali-speaking peoples (see pages 38–39).

## Survival of traditional ways

Ways of life of East Africa's inhabitants change with the varied climatic conditions. There are nomadic herders and cattle-keepers. The majority are farmers growing maize, millet, and vegetables, who also keep some cattle, sheep, and goats. Cash crops such as tea, coffee, and cotton are grown with success on peasant smallholdings.

Social groupings range from small bands of herders to farmers like the Kikuyu in Kenya who have elders, and kingdoms that have hereditary chiefs and royal families, for example, the Ganda of Uganda with their ruler the Kabaka.

To the west and southwest of Lake Victoria in present-day Uganda and Tanzania are a group of traditional kingdoms: Buganda, Toro, Bunyoro, Buhaya, and others. The peoples of this area eat bananas and plantains, rather than maize, as their main food.

Kenya, where during the colonial period there were many white settler-farmers, inherited a particularly good road–rail system, which has continued to aid its relatively prosperous development. Economic growth in Uganda and Tanzania has been limited by the problems faced by these countries. Civil war took place in Uganda in the 1970s, and in Tanzania frequent drought and long distances have resulted in poor communications. In 1994 Rwanda experienced one of the worst genocides in history.

◀ Zanzibar, "the clove island," was the 19th-century traveler's doorway into East Africa. In 1829 the Sultan of Oman transferred his capital here. It contained the main slave market. Its long Middle East connections show in the tall houses along narrow streets, with balconies from which secluded Muslim women can peep out.

### East Africa since 1945

**1945:** Britain is the main colonial power in the area.

**1952–56: Kenya** Mau-Mau uprising. Intertribal tension and resentment against European settlers causes violence.

**1961: Tanzania** Tanganyika, led by Dr. Julius Nyerere, becomes independent: joins with island of Zanzibar in 1964 to become Tanzania.

**1962: Uganda** Gains independence from Britain. Kabaka (king) of Buganda becomes head of state. **Burundi and Rwanda** These two small states gain independence.

**1963: Kenya** Gains independence from Britain.

**1966: Uganda** Constitution suspended. Prime Minister Obote overthrows Kabaka and ends role of kingdoms.

**1967: Tanzania** Nyerere issues the Arusha Declaration in which he sets out his aim for Tanzanian development and self-reliance.

**1971: Uganda** Obote overthrown by General Idi Amin.

**1971–79: Uganda** Amin rules Uganda with a reign of terror: up to 300,000 Ugandans killed by his secret police.

**1972–73: Burundi** Violence between Hutu and Tutsi peoples kills thousands. Order restored. Burundi develops close economic links with Rwanda and Democratic Republic of the Congo.

**1972: Kenya** Failed coup attempt.

**1978: Kenya** Arap Moi becomes president.

**1979: Uganda** Amin overthrown after invasion of Tanzania fails.

**1980: Uganda** Obote reelected as president but civil war continues for four years in wake of Amin's brutality.

**1993: Burundi** President Melchior Ndadaye assassinated, plunging the country into civil war.

**1994: Rwanda** 500,000—1 million civilians, most of them from the minority Tutsi group, murdered by Hutu militias.

**2005: Burundi** Pierre Nkurunziza is the first democratically elected president since beginning of civil war in 1993.

▶ Much of East Africa lies between 3,300 ft (1,000 m) and 6,600 ft (2,000 m) above sea level. There are several areas of mountainous country, and this region contains the two highest peaks in Africa: Mount Kilimanjaro (19,341 ft/ 5,895 m) and Mount Kenya (17,061 ft/5,200 m). Both are volcanoes. The Great Rift Valley (see page 10) stretches from Kenya into Tanzania, and contains several lakes, some of them salty (Lake Natron).

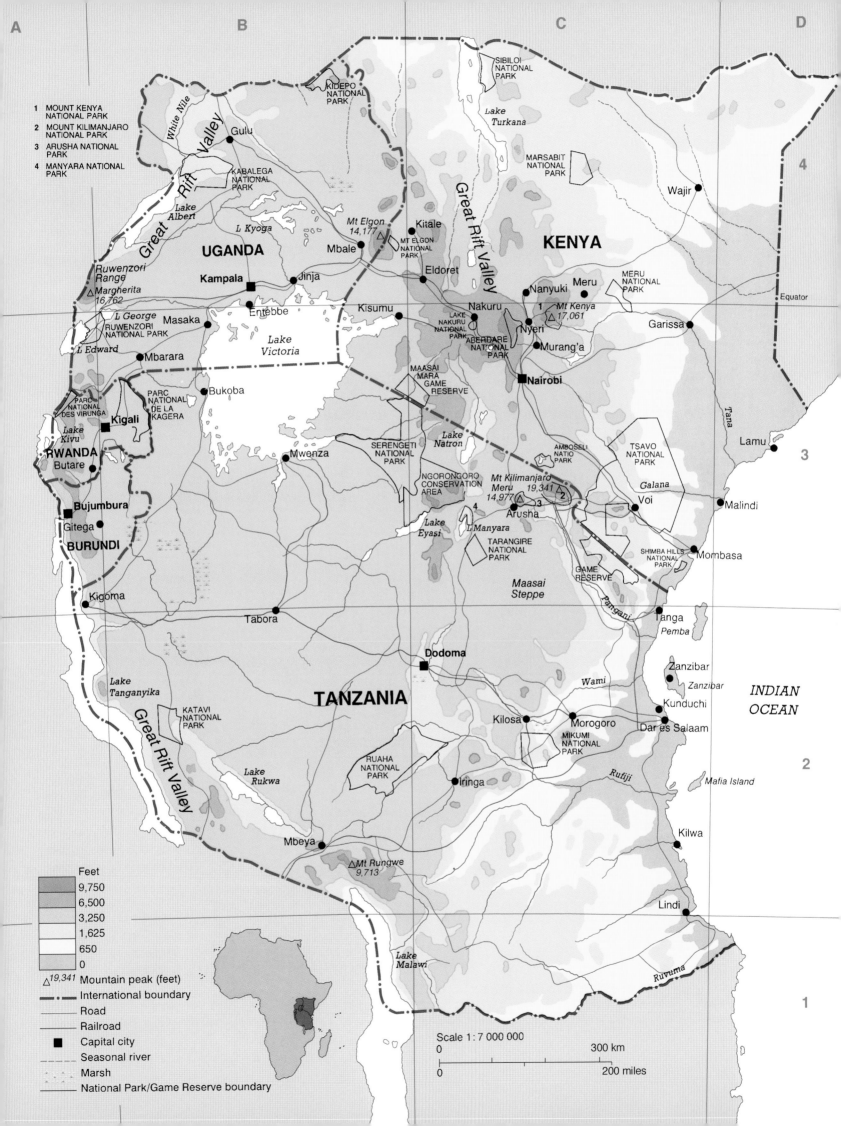

A B C D

1 MOUNT KENYA
  NATIONAL PARK
2 MOUNT KILIMANJARO
  NATIONAL PARK
3 ARUSHA NATIONAL
  PARK
4 MANYARA NATIONAL
  PARK

SIBILOI
NATIONAL
PARK

KIDEPO
NATIONAL
PARK

Gulu

White Nile

Great Rift Valley

Lake Albert

KABALEGA
NATIONAL
PARK

L Kyoga

Lake Turkana

MARSABIT
NATIONAL
PARK

Wajir

Mt Elgon
14,177

Kitale

MT ELGON
NATIONAL
PARK

Great Rift Valley

KENYA

UGANDA

Mbale

Eldoret

MERU
NATIONAL
PARK

Ruwenzori
Range

△ Margherita
16,762

L George
RUWENZORI
NATIONAL PARK

Kampala

Jinja

Kisumu

Nakuru

Nanyuki

Meru

1 △ Mt Kenya
17,061

Entebbe

LAKE
NAKURU
NATIONAL
PARK

Nyeri

Garissa

Equator

L Edward

Masaka

Mbarara

Lake
Victoria

ABERDARE
NATIONAL
PARK

Murang'a

Lamu

PARC
NATIONAL
DES VIRUNGA

PARC
NATIONAL
DE LA
KAGERA

Bukoba

MAASAI
MARA
GAME
RESERVE

Nairobi ■

Tana

Kigali ■

Lake
Kivu

RWANDA

Butare

Mwenza

SERENGETI
NATIONAL
PARK

Lake
Natron

AMBOSELI
NATIO PARK

TSAVO
NATIONAL
PARK

Bujumbura ■

Gitega

BURUNDI

NGORONGORO
CONSERVATION
AREA

Mt Kilimanjaro
Meru      19,341
14,977  △
          3 △
        2

Voi

Malindi

4

Lake
Eyasi

Arusha

L Manyara

SHIMBA HILLS
NATIONAL
PARK

Mombasa

Kigoma

TARANGIRE
NATIONAL
PARK

Maasai
Steppe

GAME
RESERVE

Pangani

Tanga

Pemba

Tabora

Dodoma ■

Wami

Zanzibar

Zanzibar

INDIAN
OCEAN

Lake
Tanganyika

TANZANIA

Kunduchi

KATAVI
NATIONAL
PARK

Kilosa

Morogoro

Dar es Salaam

Mafia Island

Lake
Rukwa

RUAHA
NATIONAL
PARK

MIKUMI
NATIONAL
PARK

Rufiji

Iringa

Kilwa

Mbeya

△ Mt Rungwe
9,713

Feet
9,750
6,500
3,250
1,625
650
0

Lindi

Lake
Malawi

Ruvuma

△ 19,341  Mountain peak (feet)

          International boundary

          Road

          Railroad

■         Capital city

          Seasonal river

          Marsh

          National Park/Game Reserve boundary

Scale 1 : 7 000 000

0                    300 km

0              200 miles

# The Game Parks of East Africa

THE REMOVAL OF TROPICAL FORESTS and the spread of agriculture, together with erosion caused by overgrazing of cattle, has caused the loss of much of the habitat of African wildlife. It decreased sharply in the 20th century. Nevertheless, Africa remains the home of many of the world's more spectacular animal species. This is largely due to the great parks which have existed for almost a century (see map page 77).

The parks' function has changed greatly in recent years. Originally they were established to shelter and protect wildlife from people—from big game hunting for sport as much as from the local population who then lost their supplies of "bushmeat." But the removal of humans as predators has sometimes meant an increase in the number of certain species, which has upset the natural balance.

## Change in the use of game parks

Increasingly game parks are being seen not as areas that should be sealed off from all outside influences, but as areas to be used and managed like any other part of the country.

For example, it is now understood that a mixed wildlife population uses the vegetable resources

◀ Since firearms are available and there has been a ready market for (sometimes illegal) wildlife products, poaching has remained a problem and has led to violence against tourists as well. Elephant and rhino are the main targets. Those who actually do the killing are just one link in the chain of people receiving profit from the trade.

◀ In 1950 the enlarging of Lake Kariba by the new Kariba Dam (on the Zambian–Zimbabwean border) led to "Operation Noah," a game rescue operation that became world famous. As the waters rose, animals were stranded on fast-disappearing islands. Having first been tranquilized, animals were transported to the new shoreline.

▶ Within the escarpment boundaries of the Rift Valley, which runs down into central Tanzania, huge herds of game —antelope, wildebeest, and many others—can still be seen. These plains are also home to the Maasai cattle herds on which they depend for their main foods: milk, blood, and occasional meat. Maasai seldom eat grain.

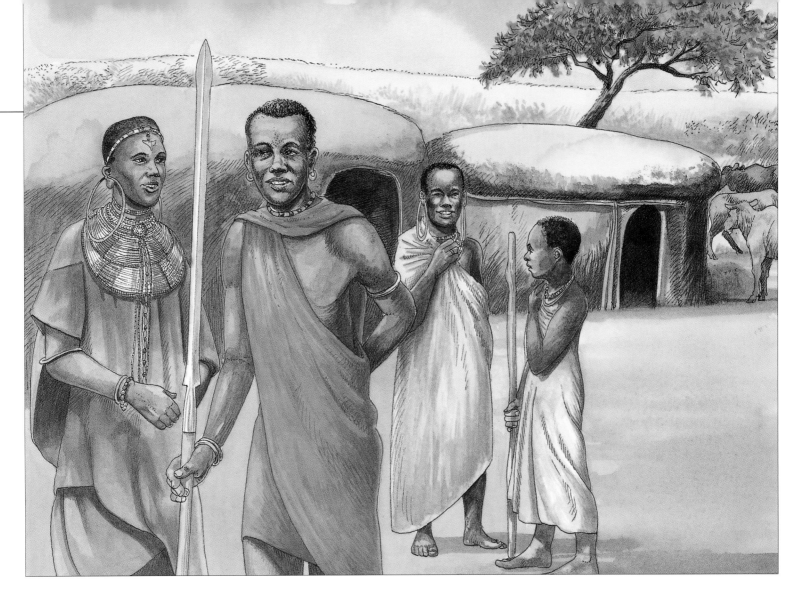

▲ A Maasai family in their homestead of low-built mud-and-stick houses. Their dress, which used to be made of leather, is now reddish tan cloth—the color of leather. Today Maasai herdsmen share the plains with game and with tourists. Traditionally the men and boys move with the herds, leaving the women and young children at home.

available more efficiently than a single species. Therefore, culling wildlife may produce more animal protein for the local human population than using the same land for a cattle ranch.

Game parks play an increasingly important part in the national economy through tourism, and they may also be used for controlled fishing, limited grazing, and planning new forests.

## Game parks and the Maasai

The existence of game parks still raises great problems for people such as the Maasai, however. Their traditional way of life, with their hunting and their cattle-keeping is under threat. Six of Kenya's and Tanzania's national parks alone cover more than 5,000 square miles (13,000 square kilometers) of what was once Maasai land.

The Maasai now have some permanent water supplies, and some of them have settled on small ranches around the fringes of the national parks. A large number of Maasai men find compatible work as game scouts. But they no longer have the freedom to roam with their cattle wherever they wish, nor to hunt wild animals. There is a danger that modern tourism will turn the Maasai into a mere spectacle.

# S.E. Central Africa

MALAWI, ZAMBIA, AND ZIMBABWE (formerly Nyasaland, Northern Rhodesia, and Southern Rhodesia) were for a short time united in the Central African Federation, a British colony. Zimbabwe has had a troubled history as a former British colony where self-government was granted to the white minority. After a bitter civil war between white settlers and African nationalists it became independent under black majority rule in 1980. A legacy of colonial rule has recently brought renewed instability.

The fourth nation in southeast central Africa, the former Portuguese colony of Mozambique, also had a period of troubles leading up to its independence in 1975. Throughout these four countries almost all the African peoples speak one or other of the Bantu languages, and share similar ways of life.

There are Muslims along the coast and in some inland regions, but in general the people still follow traditional religions or are Christians. Apart from some large organized chiefdoms (such as Barotseland), most communities were small and directed by headmen.

Cash crops such as tobacco, tea, coffee, cotton, and rice are important. In northern Zambia there is wealth from the mining of minerals in the Copper Belt (see pages 84–85). With the availability of hydroelectric power from river dams, the whole region, given political stability, may look to a prosperous future.

◀ The Victoria Falls, on the Zambezi River between Zambia and Zimbabwe, plunge 330 ft (100 m) into a narrow chasm. They were named by English explorer David Livingstone. Their African name is *Mosu-oa-tun-ya*, "smoke that thunders."

## Southeast central Africa since 1953

**1953:** Creation of Federation of Rhodesia and Nyasaland, a self-governing colony dominated by white settlers in Rhodesia.

**1964: Zambia, Malawi** Zambia (formerly Northern Rhodesia) and Malawi (formerly Nyasaland) independent after breakup of Federation in 1963. Mozambique War breaks out between white settlers backed by Portuguese army and black nationalist movements.

**1965: Southern Rhodesia** Declares its independence from Britain. A white-dominated country led by Ian Smith.

**1972–79: Southern Rhodesia** Civil war develops between settlers and black nationalist movements based in neighboring countries.

**1974: Mozambique** Portuguese resistance collapses—leads to revolution in Portugal itself.

**1975: Mozambique** Independence. **Zambia** Railway to Tanzania's coast, built with Chinese funds, is completed.

**1979: Southern Rhodesia (Zimbabwe)** Lancaster House agreement ends Rhodesian civil war. Power to be handed over to black majority after elections.

**1980: Zimbabwe** Robert Mugabe elected as Prime Minister.

**2002: Zimbabwe** Mugabe reelected to power but accused of rigging the results. Seizures of white-owned land leads to economic crisis and an estimated 5 million people in need of aid.

**2005: Zimbabwe** Mugabe demolishes "illegal" homes, leaving an estimated 700,000 urban poor homeless.

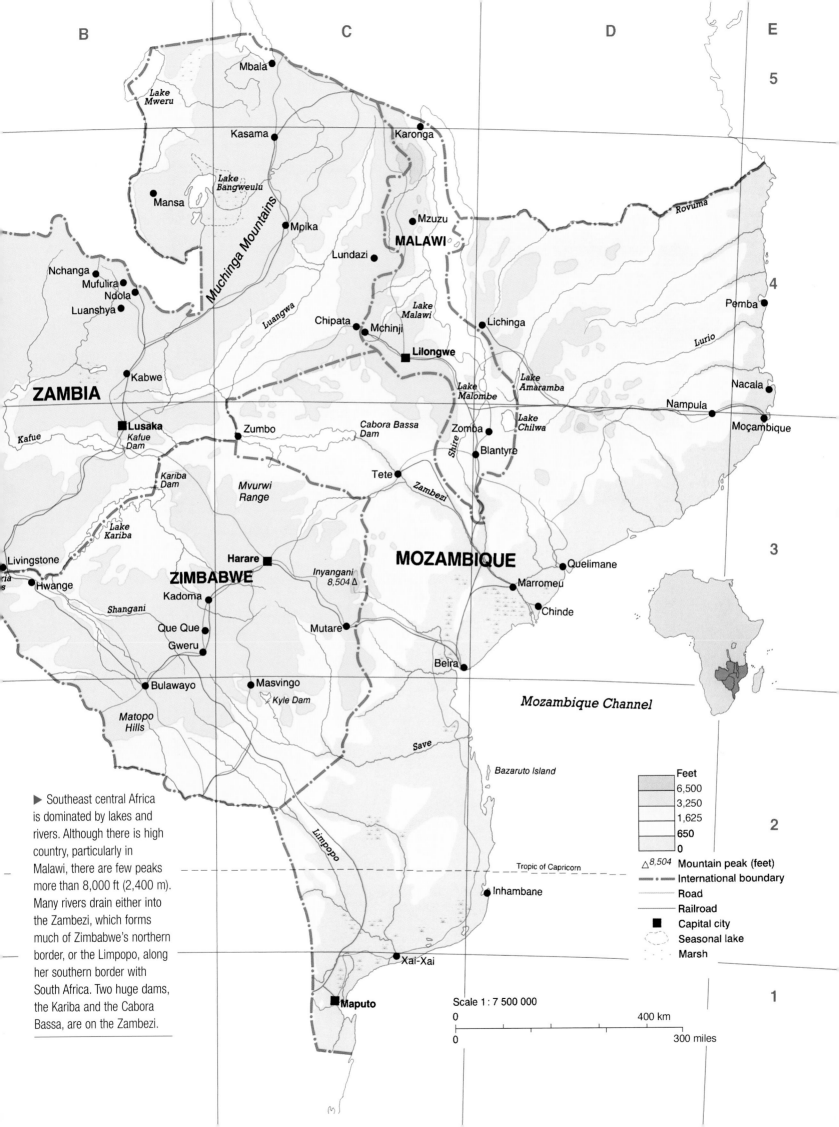

B                      C                      D              E

5

Mbala

*Lake Mweru*

Kasama

Karonga

*Lake Bangweulu*

Mansa

Mpika

Mzuzu

**MALAWI**

*Rovuma*

4

Nchanga

Lundazi

Mufulira

Ndola

Luanshya

*Muchinga Mountains*

*Luangwa*

Chipata

Mchinji

*Lake Malawi*

Lichinga

Pemba

*Lurio*

Kabwe

**ZAMBIA**

Lilongwe

*Lake Amaramba*

Nacala

Nampula

*Kafue*

**Lusaka**

*Kafue Dam*

Zumbo

*Cabora Bassa Dam*

Zomba

*Lake Malombe*

*Lake Chilwa*

Moçambique

*Kariba Dam*

*Mvurwi Range*

Blantyre

*Shire*

Tete

*Zambezi*

*Lake Kariba*

Livingstone

**ZIMBABWE**

**Harare**

*Inyangani 8,504 △*

**MOZAMBIQUE**

Quelimane

3

Hwange

Kadoma

Marromeu

*Shangani*

Chinde

Que Que

Mutare

Gweru

Beira

Bulawayo

Masvingo

*Kyle Dam*

*Mozambique Channel*

*Matopo Hills*

*Save*

*Bazaruto Island*

| | Feet |
|---|---|
| | 6,500 |
| | 3,250 |
| | 1,625 |
| | 650 |
| | 0 |

▶ Southeast central Africa is dominated by lakes and rivers. Although there is high country, particularly in Malawi, there are few peaks more than 8,000 ft (2,400 m). Many rivers drain either into the Zambezi, which forms much of Zimbabwe's northern border, or the Limpopo, along her southern border with South Africa. Two huge dams, the Kariba and the Cabora Bassa, are on the Zambezi.

*Limpopo*

*Tropic of Capricorn*

Inhambane

△8,504   Mountain peak (feet)
━ ·━ ·━   International boundary
────   Road
────   Railroad
■   Capital city
  Seasonal lake
  Marsh

Xai-Xai

**Maputo**

Scale 1 : 7 500 000

0                               400 km

0                             300 miles

2

1

# Zimbabwe

"**Z**IMBABWE" IN THE LANGUAGE OF THE local Shona people, means "house of the Chief." It refers to a large number of stone-walled enclosures that are found on the plateaus and hills of south central Zimbabwe. Formerly Southern Rhodesia (see pages 80–81), the country is now named for them. The largest and most spectacular of these remains is known as Great Zimbabwe.

## The history of Great Zimbabwe

The enclosures are in an area rich in gold and other metals. It seems that as early as 650 C.E. a centralized state began to develop farther south along the Limpopo Valley. Then, in the 11th century, Great Zimbabwe became prominent. Its ruler was known as the Monomutapa, and it prospered by raising crops and cattle. Later, the Shona became skilled miners and metalworkers, and sold much gold, copper, and ivory to Indian Ocean traders.

Great Zimbabwe was most probably the Monomutapa's capital, and the center of the religious life of his people. It was built over a period of perhaps 400 years, but during the 16th century, for reasons that are not clear, the ruler and his court left Great Zimbabwe.

## Western travelers visit

Portuguese traders and soldiers wrote about the great stone ruins, and a German explorer, Karl Mauch, visited them in 1871. He camped nearby for some months and became convinced that only outsiders, not the ancestors of the local Shona people, could have built such impressive walls.

In 1891 Cecil Rhodes, the South African politician and imperialist, sent an English traveler to study the ruins. He also concluded that the builders had come from outside and were perhaps Phoenicians. White settlers in Rhodesia accepted this idea. They dug among the ruins for treasure and took away objects they found there. An Ancient Ruins Company was formed by Europeans to sell their plunder, and a great deal of damage was caused to the site.

▶ This is how part of the king's residence would have looked in the 1400s (in the photo of the ruins opposite it is the large circle at the top). Near the Conical Tower (probably a grain store) the buttressed walls—16 ft (5 m) thick at their base— were decorated with a zigzag pattern. The outer wall was 825 ft (250 m) long and 32 ft (10 m) high. The expertly cut and laid stones (no mortar was used) showed the skill of the builders.

### The Shona receive recognition

In 1905, however, and again in 1929, professional archaeologists who had excavated in the Middle East came to work in Southern Rhodesia. The earlier group looked first at the smaller *zimbabwe* before beginning their work at Great Zimbabwe.

Both groups came to one conclusion: that there was no reason to think that Arabs or Phoenicians were the builders of the great stone enclosures, and every reason to think that it was the work of the same Shona people who still lived there. The Arab and Chinese pots and plates (some of it porcelain of the Ming period) that were found indicate that the kingdom was part of a long-distance trading network, exchanging goods with coastal settlements some 380 miles (600 km) away. It is no coincidence that Great Zimbabwe was built on a trade route to the coast.

▼ Most of the ruins are walls of circular or oval enclosures that seem never to have had roofs. Large boulders were incorporated in the walls. Smaller enclosures were probably for cattle, built next to thatched houses made of earth and poles.

# Mineral Resources

ALMOST ALL AFRICAN NATIONS HAVE SOME mineral resources, Many are exceedingly rich in either variety or quantity. Morocco has more than half the world's reserves of phosphate; the Democratic Republic of the Congo, best known for copper, leads the world in the production of industrial diamonds and of cobalt; Gabon has particularly large deposits of iron ore; and Sierra Leone is famous for its diamonds.

Uranium, now so valuable, is found in more than a dozen African countries but is largely unexploited. Bauxite is widely found in West Africa. Diamonds are the most widely found gemstone—others are amethysts, rubies, garnets, and emeralds.

Mineral wealth has not always in the past been an advantage to African nations. Often very little of the wealth stayed in the country, and extraction led to social problems for the workers.

Now, with nations being independent, there is hope that rich deposits may be exploited well, bringing wealth within Africa. However, the exploitation of mineral wealth to fund the ongoing civil war in the Democratic Republic of the Congo shows that it can still be misused.

## Exploiting the mineral reserves

The extraction, processing, and transportation of minerals is costly. When deposits are discovered far inland, in underpopulated areas with demanding climates, it is not surprising that many of them remain "unexploited."

The areas that have been exploited have both great quantities of minerals and access to Western money and technology. These are, particularly, the Copper Belt of Zambia and the Democratic Republic of the Congo; the diamond mines of Tanzania; South Africa's great deposits of gold on the ridge of rock, the Rand, and diamonds around the town of Kimberley; and, more recently, Namibia's coastal diamond deposits in the southwest.

## Importing labor

Most mineral extraction requires a large labor force, as well as technology. The towns and cities of the Copper Belt and the Rand have been known for their vast number of migrant laborers—African men who leave their homes and families in rural areas, sometimes in another country, and work for a contracted period in the mines. They must live in bleak prisonlike hostels, sending money to support their families. A small landlocked country such as

▲ Open-cast copper mining at Likasi, Democratic Republic of the Congo. In this country a state-owned organization controls mining and refining, although experts from overseas are still employed.

◀ Mufulira, one of a cluster of eight mining townships on the Zambian Copper Belt. These towns make extensive use of poor agricultural land for housing.

◀ Stacking paper-thin copper sheets for export. The copper is refined so that its value in relation to its bulk is high. Because Zambia is a landlocked country, the cost of transportation adds greatly to the price of its raw materials.

▶ Two large steam trains meet on the main railway link between Bloemfontein and Bethlehem in South Africa. New capital investment will eventually lead to the replacement of all steam trains in South Africa.

▲ Underground mining in the Democratic Republic of the Congo. Open-cast methods are also used.

▼ Many diamonds come from long-extinct volcanoes. Rock is drilled and crushed to release the diamonds.

Lesotho might have as many as one in eight of its male adult population absent at the mines, and the money they send home makes up a large part of the national income.

## The Copper Belt

Africa is a major producer of the world's copper, and there are copper deposits in many of its countries. The copper-mining industry in Zambia is centered on a number of mining towns (Kitwe-Nkana, Ndola, Nchanga, and others) in what is known as the Copper Belt. Copper was first mined in precolonial times, and a modern copper industry developed in the mid-1920s. Most of Zambia's export earnings come from copper.

# Southern Africa

ALTHOUGH THE COUNTRIES OF THIS REGION have their own governments, they are dominated by South Africa. Lesotho, Swaziland, and Botswana once came under British rule. Namibia (former German South West Africa) became a South African trust territory. It finally became an independent nation state in March 1990.

All the Africans of these five nations speak Bantu languages, except the Khoisan peoples of the central and southwest deserts. The Khoekhoe, of whom few are left, were cattle herders; the San and other groups were hunter-gatherers (see pages 88–89).

The first white settlers in the early 17th century were Dutch and they were joined by French and British settlers in the 18th and 19th centuries. The Dutch farmers (the Boers), in the course of their search for good land, came into conflict with Bantu-speaking peoples who already used the same type of land (see pages 26–27).

The discovery of gold and diamonds on the Rand near Johannesburg was one factor in the Anglo–Boer War of 1899–1902, a cause of continuing bitterness between the Afrikaners and the English-speaking whites. The mines use black African migrant labor from other states, and South Africa's neighbors are therefore kept economically dependent.

▶ From a narrow coastal plain the land gradually climbs to the high veld before descending to the drier lands of the Kalahari Desert. The highest land is in the landlocked kingdom of Lesotho, with mountains more than 10,000 ft (3,000 m) high. More fertile land lies in the east and extreme south.

When self-government was granted to South Africa in 1910 the majority blacks and Indians (who had been encouraged to settle to provide another labor force) were excluded from any part in government. Their exclusion, and that of people of mixed race, was the basis of apartheid, which was finally removed in the early 1990s.

## Southern Africa since 1948

**1948: South Africa** National Party comes to power. Represents white-dominated Afrikaner viewpoint.

**1960: South Africa** Massacre of demonstrators at Sharpeville.

**1961: South Africa** Leaves Commonwealth and becomes a republic. Continues policy of apartheid.

**1963: South Africa** Nelson Mandela, leader of the African National Congress (ANC), is imprisoned.

**1966: Botswana** Gains independence from Britain.

**1976:** Transkei, the first black "homeland" gains "independence," but is dependent on South Africa.

**1978: South Africa** P.W. Botha succeeds Dr. Vorster as leader.

**1985: South Africa** State of Emergency declared by government; more restrictions on press freedom.

**1989: South Africa** Dr. Botha resigns. Succeeded by more liberal F.W. de Klerk.

**1990: South Africa** Nelson Mandela released. **Namibia** Independence after years of South African control.

**1994: South Africa** ANC wins large majority in first multiracial general election. Nelson Mandela becomes first black South African president.

**1999: South Africa** Thabo Mbeki elected president.

**2001: South Africa** It is predicted that within a few years AIDS will reduce life expectancy for black people in South Africa from 60 to 40 years.

**2003: South Africa** ANC government announces rollout of AIDS drugs after internal and international pressure.

◀ Women of the Herero people, who live in western Botswana and Namibia, still wear turbans and long cotton dresses made in the style introduced by the 19th-century missionaries of the (German) Rhenish Missionary Society (see pages 30–31). The Herero are active Lutherans, and their church has been involved in Namibia's long struggle to gain independence from South Africa.

Etosha Pan

A

Ugab

**NAMIBIA**

ATLANTIC OCEAN

Swakopmund ●

Walvis Bay ●

**Windhoek**

Namib Desert

● Lüderitz

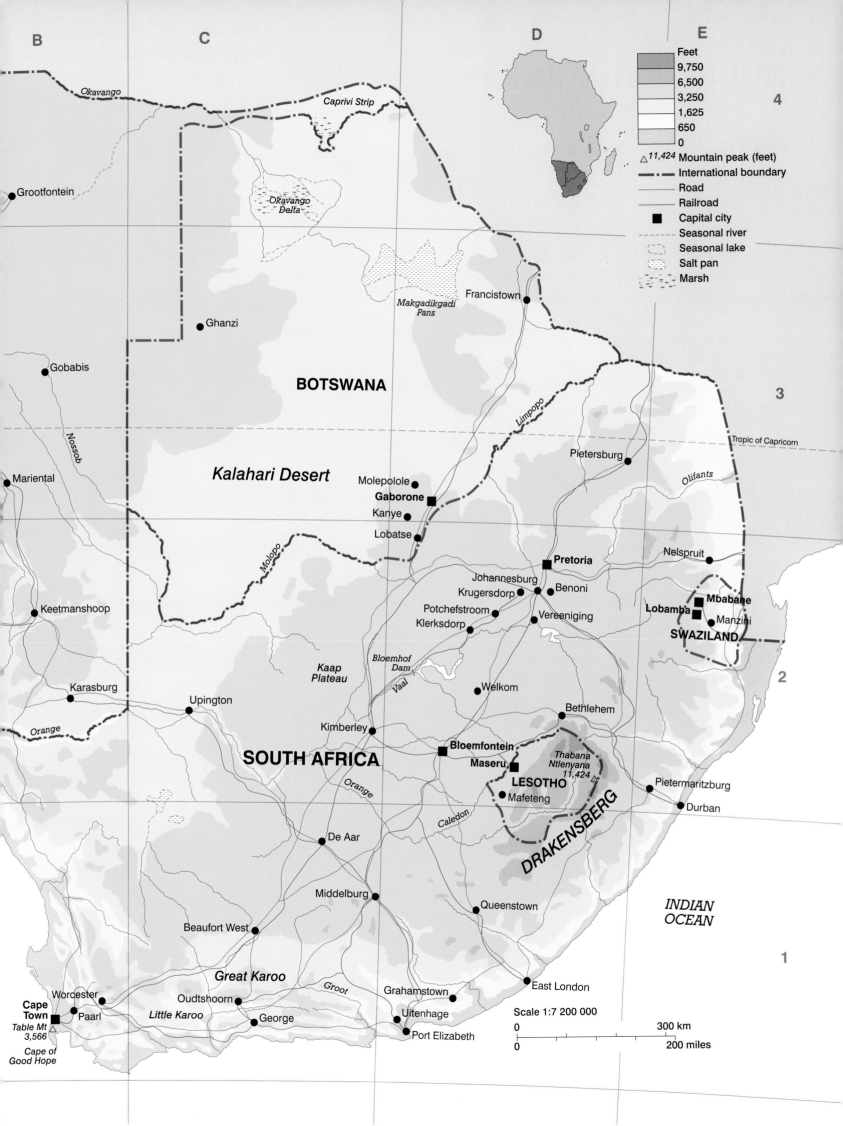

B                    C                    D                    E

4

**Feet**
9,750
6,500
3,250
1,625
650
0

△11,424 Mountain peak (feet)
International boundary
Road
Railroad
■ Capital city
Seasonal river
Seasonal lake
Salt pan
Marsh

*Okavango*

*Caprivi Strip*

Grootfontein

*Okavango Delta*

Francistown

Ghanzi

*Makgadikgadi Pans*

Gobabis

**BOTSWANA**

3

*Nossob*

*Limpopo*

Tropic of Capricorn

Mariental

*Kalahari Desert*

Pietersburg

*Olifants*

Molepolole

Kanye

**Gaborone** ■

Nelspruit

*Molopo*

Lobatse

**Pretoria** ■

**Lobamba** **Mbabane** ■

Keetmanshoop

Johannesburg

Benoni

Manzini

Krugersdorp

**SWAZILAND**

Potchefstroom

Vereeniging

Klerksdorp

2

Karasburg

*Kaap Plateau*

*Bloemhof Dam*

Welkom

Bethlehem

Upington

*Vaal*

*Orange*

Kimberley

**SOUTH AFRICA**

**Bloemfontein** ■

*Thabana Ntlenyana 11,424* △

Pietermaritzburg

**Maseru** ■

**LESOTHO**

Durban

Mafeteng

*Caledon*

**DRAKENSBERG**

De Aar

Middelburg

Queenstown

*INDIAN OCEAN*

1

Beaufort West

*Great Karoo*

East London

*Groot*

Grahamstown

Worcester

**Cape Town** ■

Paarl

Oudtshoorn

*Little Karoo*

George

Uitenhage

*Table Mt 3,566* △

Port Elizabeth

Scale 1:7 200 000

*Cape of Good Hope*

0 ———— 300 km

0 ———— 200 miles

# Hunter-gatherers

THE PEOPLE LIVING AT THE TIP OF SOUTH Africa when the first European explorers arrived were quite unlike the West Africans. They had yellowish skins and were cattle-herders, not farmers. The Dutch called them *Hottentots* (Dutch for "stutterer," because of the click sound in their speech). They called themselves *Khoekhoen*, "Men of men," and today they are known as Khoekhoe.

## The San people

Living alongside the Khoekhoen were much shorter yellow-skinned people who spoke languages of the same family as the Khoekhoe—click languages. The Khoekhoe called them San. These people, also known as Bushmen, did not plant crops or keep cattle. They hunted game and gathered wild honey, wild fruit, and roots. Otherwise, they were much like the Khoekhoe.

Over the years the San were systematically robbed of their land and culturally exterminated, except for a few remote groups in the drier country where cattle and crops do not flourish. Now most San people live in and around the Kalahari Desert in the northwest of South Africa, Namibia, and Botswana. They still try to follow the old way of life, living in small bands, without houses or shelter, finding what they want on the veld, but this way of life is fast disappearing, and

most San now live in poverty-stricken shantytown settlements. During the dry season, the San are expert at finding roots and melon fruit, which provide them with liquid as well as food.

For meat, they eat the game that the men bring back from hunting, using bow and poisoned arrows. Almost every part of the animal—skin and bones as well as meat—is used. Some men work on the farms of whites or Bantu-speaking Africans and have money to buy iron knives, cotton cloth, and tobacco.

◀ A baby is suckled by its mother. At this age it is carried on its mother's back in a *kaross*. San women try not to increase their families too soon, for if another child is born before the toddler is weaned, the unprotected child is less likely to survive.

◀ The San way of life relates back to the Stone Age. The semidesert land to which they have gradually been confined is becoming more barren every year. Drought and overgrazing by stock belonging to settled Africans extends the desert, and has led to attempts to settle the San people.

▶ A small band of San people gathering food as they move across the veld. They are picking spiny jelly melons. Some are holding digging sticks, which they use to get at juicy roots. Others carry bundles that contain their few possessions—mainly large gourds and water containers made from ostrich eggs.

# Africa in the World

SINCE THE 1950s THE COUNTRIES OF AFRICA have become independent nations. Many of the problems that the new states had to face were the result of the colonial division of Africa. On maps boundary lines were drawn that had no connection with the people who lived in the land, especially where people were used to a nomadic or seminomadic life.

Now, however, Africa's nations are all aligned in various political and economic groupings, some of them international. All of them belong to the United Nations Organization (UN).

## Membership of organizations

Except for Morocco, all African countries belong to the African Union (AU). Replacing the Organization of African Unity (OAU) in 2002, the new African Union is loosely modeled on that of the European

◄ Sugar makes up about 90 percent of Mauritius's exports. The settlers who came to the island were African slaves, Arab sailors, Chinese laborers, Indian traders, plus French and British.

▲ The local people fish in the shallow waters off Zanzibar. The island used to be the Western travelers' doorway to the continent, but today it is economically and politically separate from it.

Union (EU), and has among its aims security, stability, development, and cooperation within Africa.

The Arab League is "a voluntary organization of sovereign Arab states" that was founded in 1945 to encourage economic, cultural, and social cooperation between Arab countries. Ten of the 22 members are African, with the remaining 12 being found in the Middle East. The African members of the league form an important bridge between the nations of black Africa and those of the Arab world.

Based in Addis Ababa, Ethiopia, the Economic Commission for Africa (ECA) promotes international cooperation for African development and supports the social and economic growth of its members.

The Cotonou Agreement is another grouping that is important for the economic future of Africa. It

provides the structure for trade and cooperation between the European Union (EU) and more than 70 member states from Africa, the Caribbean, and the Pacific region.

African nations also participate in and benefit from various UN agencies. UNESCO (United Nations Educational, Scientific, and Cultural Organization), for instance, has regional headquarters in Dakar, Senegal, Cairo, Egypt, and Nairobi, Kenya. The International Labor Organization (ILO) has its regional office in Addis Ababa.

In 2005 the world's wealthiest nations launched the G8 Africa Action Plan, which is committed to peacekeeping, fighting diseases, promoting economic development, strengthening governments, and implementing debt relief in Africa.

▼ The sunny beaches of the East African coast are now havens for tourists from all over the world.

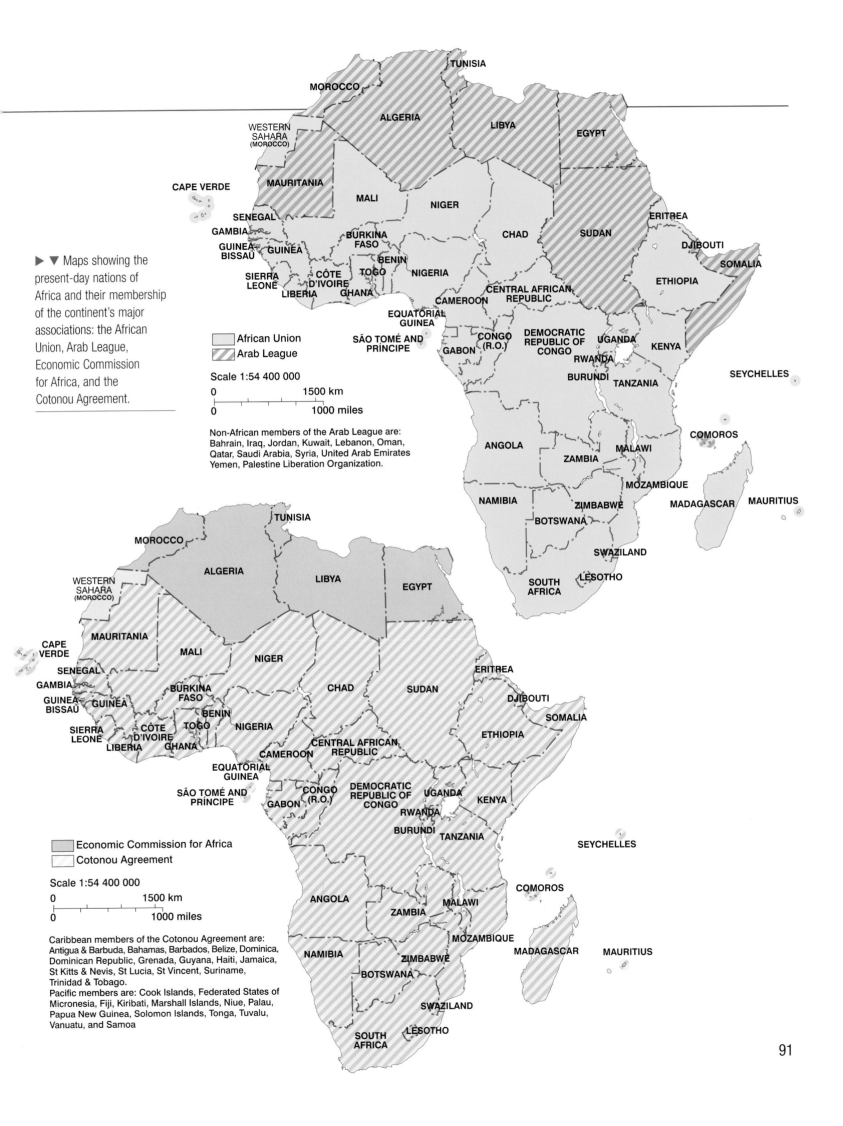

▶ ▼ Maps showing the present-day nations of Africa and their membership of the continent's major associations: the African Union, Arab League, Economic Commission for Africa, and the Cotonou Agreement.

African Union
Arab League

Scale 1:54 400 000

0 — 1500 km
0 — 1000 miles

Non-African members of the Arab League are: Bahrain, Iraq, Jordan, Kuwait, Lebanon, Oman, Qatar, Saudi Arabia, Syria, United Arab Emirates Yemen, Palestine Liberation Organization.

Economic Commission for Africa
Cotonou Agreement

Scale 1:54 400 000

0 — 1500 km
0 — 1000 miles

Caribbean members of the Cotonou Agreement are: Antigua & Barbuda, Bahamas, Barbados, Belize, Dominica, Dominican Republic, Grenada, Guyana, Haiti, Jamaica, St Kitts & Nevis, St Lucia, St Vincent, Suriname, Trinidad & Tobago.
Pacific members are: Cook Islands, Federated States of Micronesia, Fiji, Kiribati, Marshall Islands, Niue, Palau, Papua New Guinea, Solomon Islands, Tonga, Tuvalu, Vanuatu, and Samoa

91

# Glossary

**alpine plant** Plant growing on mountains above the timberline.

**broad-leaved forest** Evergreen forest of trees with wide leaves (i.e., not conifers).

**bronze** An alloy (mixture) of copper and tin (and sometimes other elements). In history, Bronze Age cultures date from about 4000 to 1600 B.C.E.

**citadel** A fortress commanding a city; a stronghold.

**clan** An extended family or group of families descended from the same pair of ancestors.

**continental plate** Section of Pangea, a vast single landmass that existed 200 million years ago. It separated into sections, or plates, that form the modern continents.

**delta** The mouth of a river, built up with alluvial deposits (sand, mud, and silt) into a triangular shape, like a Greek capital D, "delta" (Δ).

**dhow** (Arabic) Sailing boat with a high poop, now used as a general term for many types of boats that used the monsoon winds to sail from the Indian sub-continent or Arabian peninsula to East African coastal ports.

**diviner** Religious official (often a priest) who interprets present happenings (illnesses and so on), and foretells the future by looking at signs (such as the way stones or nuts fall on a special tray).

**eland** (Afrikaans) Large African antelope with short spirally twisted horns (in males and females).

**fault** A break or area of fracture, usually with reference to a layer of rock. Movements of adjacent rock occur around such breaks and a number of them form a fault system.

**fossil** Remains (bone, wood, and so on) of animals, vegetables, or humans, preserved in earth or rock, usually for very long periods.

**French Foreign Legion** Several companies of non-French soldiers but with French officers, mainly serving in overseas French colonies, especially in North Africa (Morocco, Tunisia, Algeria).

**hinterland** Region beyond a coast, often linked to the coast in providing supplies.

**Iron Age** Period of human culture (from about 1600 to 1000 B.C.E.) when people learned to smelt iron and to make and use iron tools.

**Islam** The religion founded in the Arabian peninsula by the prophet Muhammad in the early seventh century C.E. It declares that there is no god but Allah and that Muhammad is the Messenger of Allah. Its holy book is the Koran and its followers are known as Muslims.

**lichen** Any one of a number of plants made up of the association of algae and fungi. Lichens grow on a solid surface, such as a rock.

**mandate** Territory (in this book refers to a former German colony) entrusted by one power to another (here the League of Nations and a member nation) to govern responsibly.

**metal-casting** Giving shape to a substance by pouring molten metal into a form or mold.

**missionary** Person sent on a special service or mission; used of religious preachers/teachers sent by one church to preach and teach in another country.

**Muslim** A person who follows the Islamic religion.

**oracle** Wise message about the future given by a diviner such as a priest or god.

**protectorate** Territory (often conquered) ruled by one power at the request of another. The term was used after World War II of former German and Italian colonies, some of which were previously known as mandates.

**rift system** A series of fault lines that have resulted in long breaks in the Earth's crust, with very high and abrupt drops to valley floors. Many are on the ocean floors, but the African rift system, one of the largest in the world, runs from the Red Sea to southern Africa.

**savanna** (Spanish) Treeless plain. The term was originally used in tropical America but now usually refers to the vast open grasslands of East Africa.

**shantytown** A poor and depressed area with inadequate housing.

**Stone Age** First known period of human culture, when stone tools were used. It dates from about 10,000 to 4000 B.C.E.

**UNESCO** Abbreviation of United Nations Educational, Scientific, and Cultural Organization.

**veld** (Dutch) Wild grassland with scattered trees, especially in southern Africa.

---

## FURTHER READING

### Books for adults

Appiah, K. A., and H. L. Gates. *Africana: The Encyclopedia of the African and African American Experience* (Oxford University Press, 2005).

Arnold, G. *Africa: A Modern History* (Atlantic Books, 2005).

Beckwith, C., Fisher, A., and G. Hancock. *African Ark: People and Ancient Cultures of Ethiopia and the Horn of Africa* (Harry N. Abrams, 1990).

Davidson, B. *Africa in History: Themes and Outlines* (Orion, 2001).

Deacon, H. J., and J. Deacon. *Human Beginnings in South Africa: Uncovering the Secrets of the Stone Age* (Altmira Press, 1999).

July, R. W. *A History of the African People* (Waveland Press, 1997).

Mandela, N. *Long Walk to Freedom: The Autobiography of Nelson Mandela* (Holt, Rinehart & Winston, 2000).

Meredith, M. *The Fate of Africa: From the Hopes of Freedom to the Fate of Despair* (Public Affairs, 2005).

Phillipson, D. *African Archaeology*, 3rd edition (Cambridge University Press, 2005).

Sparks, A. *Beyond the Miracle: Inside the New South Africa* (University of Chicago Press, 2004).

Thompson, L. *A History of South Africa* (Yale University Press, 2001).

### Books for young people

Ayo, Y. *Eyewitness: Africa* (Dorling Kindersley, 2000).

Hynson, C. *Exploration of Africa* (Econo-Clad, 2001).

MacDonald, F., and G. Wood. *Ancient African Town* (Franklin Watts, 1998).

McKissack, P., and F. McKissack. *The Royal Kingdoms of Ghana, Mali, and Songhay: Life in Medieval Africa* (Henry Holt and Co., 1995).

Naidoo, B. *No Turning Back: A Novel of South Africa* (HarperTrophy, 1999).

Richardson, H. *Life in Ancient Africa* (Crabtree, 2005).

Sheehan, S. *South Africa Since Apartheid* (Hodder Wayland, 2002).

Thomas, V. M. *Lest We Forget: The Passage from Africa to Slavery and Emancipation* (Crown, 1997).

van Beek, W. E. A. *Dogon: Africa's People of the Cliffs* (Harry N. Abrams, 2001).

### Useful Web sites

http://www.allafrica.com
Information on current political, economic, and social events in Africa.

http:www.mnh.si.edu/africanvoices
The Smithsonian Institution African Voices exhibition.

http://www.nationalgeographic.com/africa
The National Geographic Africa series Web site.

http://pbs.org/africa
The Public Broadcasting Service Web site takes you on a virtual tour of Africa.

# Gazetteer

The gazetteer lists places and features, such as islands or rivers, found on the maps. Each has a separate entry including a page and grid reference number. For example:
Aswan 53 J2

All features are shown in *italic* type. For example:
*Atbara, r.* 11 F6, 73 D5

A letter after the feature describes the kind of feature:
*i.* island; *isls.* islands;
*r.* river; *mt.* mountain;
*mts.* mountains

*Abaya, Lake* 73 D3
*Abbe, Lake* 73 E4
Abéché 68 C6
Abeokuta 59 E2
Abidjan 11 B5, 59 D2
Abuja 11 C5, 59 F2
Accra 11 B5, 59 D2
*Adamawa Highlands* 59 G2
Addis Ababa 11 F5, 73 D2
*Aden, Gulf of* 11 G6, 73 F4
Adigrat 73 D4
Agades 59 F4
*Air, mts.* 11 C6, 59 F4
*Akosombo Dam* 59 E2
*Albert, Lake* 11 F5, 68 E4, 77 B4
Alexandria 53 I3
Algiers 11 C8, 52 E4
Al Jawf 53 H2
*Amaramba, Lake* 81 D4
Annaba 52 F4
Antananarivo 11 G3
*Arabian Desert* 11 F7, 53 J2
Arusha 77 C3
Asmara 11 F6,73 D5
Assab 73 E4
Aswan 53 J2
*Aswan Dam* 53 J1
Asyut 53 J2
Atbara 73 C5
*Atbara, r.* 11 F6, 73 D5
*Atlas Mountains* 11 C7, 52 D3
Axum 73 D4

Bamako 10 B6, 58 C3
Bambari 68 C4
*Bandiagara Plateau* 59 D3
Bandundu 68 B3
Bangui 11 D5, 68 C4
*Bangweulu, Lake* 81 B4
Banjul 10 A6, 58 A3
Bata 68 A4
*Batu, mt.* 73 D3
Bawiti 53 I2
Baydhabo 73 E2

*Bazaruto Island* 81 D2
Beaufort West 87 C1
Bechar 52 D3
Beida 53 H3
Beira 81 C3
Benghazi 53 H3
Benguela 68 B1
Béni Abbès 52 D3
*Benin, Bight of* 59 E2
Benin City 59 F2
Benoni 87 D2
*Benue, r.* 11 C5, 59 F2
Berbera 73 F4
Berberati 68 B4
Bethlehem 87 D2
*Bié Plateau* 11 D3, 68 B2
*Bioko, i.* 11 C5, 68 A4
Bissau 10 A6, 58 A3
Bizerte 53 F4
*Black Volta, r.* 59 D2
Blantyre 81 D3
Bloemfontein 87 D2
*Bloemhof Dam* 87 D2
*Blue Nile, r.* 11 F6, 73 C4
Bo 58 B2
*Boa Vista, i.* 58 I7
Bobo Dioulasso 59 D3
*Bodélé Depression* 11 B8, 68 B6
Bondo 68 C4
Bouaké 59 C2
Bouar 68 B4
Bouârfa 52 D3
*Brava, i.* 58 I7
Brazzaville 11 D4, 68 B3
Buchanan 58 C2
*Bui Dam* 59 D2
Bujumbura 11 E4, 77 A3
Bukavu 68 D3
Bukoba 77 B3
Bulawayo 81 B2
Bumba 68 C4
Burco 73 F3
Buta 68 D4
Butare 77 A3

Cabinda 11 D4, 68 B3
*Cabora Bassa Dam* 81 C3
Cairo 11 F8, 53 J3
*Caledon, r.* 87 D1
*Cameroon, Mount* 11 C5, 59 F1
*Canary Islands* 10 A7, 52 B2
Cape Town 87 B1
Casablanca 52 C3
*Catherine, Mount* 53 J2
Ceuta 52 D3
*Chad, Lake* 11 D6, 59 G3, 68 B6
*Chari, r.* 11 D6, 68 B5
*Chilwa, Lake* 81 D3
Chinde 81 D3
Chipata 81 C4
*Choke Mountains* 73 D4
*Comoe, r.* 59 D2
Conakry 10 A6, 58 B2

*Congo, r.* 11 D4, 11 E5, 68 B3, 68 C4
*Congo Basin* 11 D4
Constantine 52 F4
Cotonou 59 E2
*Cuando, r.* 68 C1
*Cuanza, r.* 68 B2
*Cubango, r.* 11 D3, 68 B1
*Cuito, r.* 68 C1

*Dahlak Archipelago, isls.* 73 E5
Dakar 10 A6, 58 A3
Dakhla 52 B1
Daloa 59 C2
*Danakil Depression* 73 E4
Dar es Salaam 77 C2
*Darfur* 72 A4
*Dawa, r.* 73 E2
De Aar 87 C1
Debre Markos 73 D4
Dese 73 D4
Dire Dawa 73 E3
Djibouti 11 G6, 73 E4
Dodoma 11 F4, 77 C2
Douala 59 F1
*Drakensberg, mts.* 11 E1, 87 D1
Durban 87 E2

East London 87 D1
*Edward, Lake* 68 D3, 77 A3
El Aaiun 10 A7, 52 B2
Eldoret 77 C4
El Faiyum 53 J2
El Fasher 72 B4
El Giza 53 J2
El Kharga 53 J2
El Obeid 72 C4
*Elgon, Mount* 11 F5, 77 B4
*Emi Koussi, mt.* 11 D6, 68 C7
En Nahud 72 B4
Entebbe 77 B4
Enugu 59 F2
Er Roseires 73 C4
*Ethiopian Highlands* 11 F5, 73 D3
*Etosha Pan* 86 B4
*Eyasi, Lake* 77 C3

Faya-Largeau 68 C6
Fderik 58 B5
Fès 52 D3
*Fogo, i.* 58 I7
*Fouta Djallon, mts.* 10 A6, 58 B3
Franceville 68 B3
Francistown 87 D3
Freetown 10 A5, 58 B2
*Fuerteventura, i.* 52 B2

Gabes 53 F3
Gaborone 11 D2, 87 D3
*Gambia, r.* 10 A6, 58 B3
Gao 59 D4
Garissa 77 C3

Garoua 59 G2
Gedaref 73 D4
George 87 C1
*George, Lake* 77 B3
Ghanzi 87 C3
Gitega 77 A3
Gobabis 87 B3
*Gomera, i.* 52 B2
Gonder 73 D4
*Good Hope, Cape of* 11 D1, 87 B1
Gore 73 D3
Grahamstown 87 D1
*Gran Canaria, i.* 52 B2
*Great Karoo, mts.* 11 E1, 87 C1
*Great Rift Valley* 77 B4
*Groot, r.* 87 C1
Grootfontein 87 B4
*Guardafui, Cape* 11 H6
*Guinea, Gulf of* 11 B5, 59 E1
Gulu 77 B4
*Guna, mt.* 73 D4
Gweru 81 B3

Harare 11 F3, 81 C3
Harer 73 E3
Hargeysa 73 E3
*Hierro, i.* 52 A2
*High Atlas, mts.* 52 C3
Hobyo 73 F3
*Hoggar, mts.* 11 C7, 52 E1
Huambo 68 B1
Hwange 81 B3

Ibadan 59 E2
Ife 59 E2
Igbo-Ukwe 59 F2
Ilebo 68 C3
Ilorin 59 E2
Impfondo 68 B4
*Inga Dam* 68 B3
Inhambane 81 D2
*Inyangani, mt.* 81 C3
Iringa 77 C2
Isiro 68 D4
*Ituri Forest* 68 D4

Jima 73 D3
Jinja 77 B4
Johannesburg 87 D2
*Jonglei Canal* 11 F1, 73 C3
*Jos Plateau* 59 F3
Juba 73 C3
*Juba, r.* 11 G5, 73 E2

*Kaap Plateau* 87 C2
*Kabompo, r.* 80 A4
Kabwe 81 B4
Kadoma 81 B3
Kaduna 59 F3
*Kafue, r.* 81 B3
*Kafue Dam* 81 B3
*Kainji Dam* 59 E2
*Kainji Reservoir* 59 E3
*Kalahari Desert* 11 E2, 87 C3

Kalemie 68 D2
Kamina 68 D2
Kampala 11 F5, 77 B4
Kananga 68 C3
Kankan 58 C3
Kano 59 F3
Kanye 87 D3
Kaolack 58 A3
Karasburg 87 B2
*Kariba, Lake* 11 E3, 81 B3
*Kariba Dam* 81 B3
Karonga 81 C4
*Kasai, r.* 11 D4, 68 C2
Kasama 81 C4
Kassala 73 D5
Katsina 59 F3
Kayes 58 B3
Keetmanshoop 87 B2
*Kenya, Mount* 11 F5, 77 C3
Khartoum 11 F6, 73 C5
Khartoum North 73 C5
Kigali 11 E4, 77 B3
Kigoma 77 A3
Kikwit 68 C3
*Kilimanjaro, Mount* 11 F4, 77 C3
Kilosa 77 C2
Kilwa 77 C2
Kimberley 87 C2
Kindu 68 D3
Kinshasa 11 D4, 68 B3
Kisangani 68 D4
Kismaayo 73 E1
Kisumu 77 B3
Kitale 77 C4
*Kivu, Lake* 68 D3, 77 A3
Klerksdorp 87 D2
*Kossoul Dam* 59 C2
Kosti 73 C4
Krugersdorp 87 D2
Kumasi 59 D2
Kunduchi 77 C2
*Kwango, r.* 11 D4, 68 B2
*Kyle Dam* 81 C2
*Kyoga, Lake* 11 F5, 77 B4

Labe 58 B3
Lagos 59 E2
Lalibela 73 D4
Lambaréné 68 A3
Lamu 77 D3
*Lanzarote, i.* 52 B2
Léré 68 B5
Libreville 11 C5, 68 A4
*Libyan Desert* 11 E7, 53 I2
*Libyan Plateau* 53 I3
Lichinga 81 D4
Likasi 68 D2
Lilongwe 11 F3, 81 C4
*Limpopo, r.* 11 F2, 81 C2, 87 D3
Lindi 77 C2
*Little Karoo, mts.* 87 C1
Livingstone 81 B3
Lobamba 11 F2, 87 E2
Lobatse 87 D2

93

Lobito 68 B1
Logone, r. 68 B5
Lomami, r. 11 E4, 68 D3
Lomé 11 C5, 59 E2
Loubomo 68 B3
Lualaba, r. 11 E4, 68 D3
Luanda 11 D4, 68 B2
Luangwa, r. 81 C4
Luanshya 81 B4
Lubango 68 B1
Lubumbashi 68 D2
Lüderitz 86 B2
Lulua, r. 68 C2
Lundazi 81 C4
Lusaka 11 E3, 81 B3
Luuq 73 E2

Madeira, isls. 10 A8, 52 B3
Mafeteng 87 D2
Mafia Island 77 C2
Maiduguri 59 G3
Mai-Ndombe, Lake 68 C3
Maio, i. 58 I7
Makgadikgadi Pans 11 E2, 87 D3
Malabo 11 C5, 68 A4
Malakal 73 C3
Malanje 68 B2
Malawi, Lake 11 F3, 77 B1, 81 C4
Malindi 77 D3
Malombe, Lake 81 D4
Man 58 C2
Mansa 81 B4
Manyara, Lake 77 E3
Manzini 87 E2
Maputo 11 F2, 81 C1
Margherita, mt. 77 A4
Mariental 87 B3
Marka 73 E2
Maroua 59 G3
Marrah, Jabal, mt. 11 E6, 72 A4
Marrakesh 52 C3
Marromeu 81 D3
Masaka 77 B3
Maseru 11 E2, 87 D2
Massawa 73 D5
Masvingo 81 C2
Matadi 68 B3
Matopo Hills 81 B2
Mbabane 11 F2, 87 E2
Mbala 81 C5
Mbale 77 B4
Mbandaka 68 C4

Mbarara 77 B3
Mbeya 77 B2
Mbuji-Mayi 68 C2
Mchinji 81 C4
Mediterranean Sea 11 E8, 53 H3
Meknes 52 D3
Melilla 52 D3
Mendebo Mountains 73 D3
Merowe 73 C5
Meru 77 C4
Meru, mt. 77 C3
Middelburg 87 C1
Misratah 53 G3
Moçambique 81 E3
Mogadishu 11 G5, 73 F2
Molepolole 87 D3
Molopo, r. 87 C2
Mombasa 77 C3
Mongu 80 A3
Monrovia 10 A5, 58 B2
Mopti 59 D3
Morogoro 77 C2
Moroni 11 G3
Mozambique Channel 11 F3, 81 D2
Mpika 81 C4
Muchinga Mountains 81 C4
Mufulira 81 B4
Murang'a 77 C3
Mutare 81 C3
Mvurwi Range, mts. 81 C3
Mwenza 77 B3
Mweru, Lake 11 E4, 68 D2, 81 B5
Mzuzu 81 C4

Nacala 81 E4
Nairobi 11 F4, 77 C3
Nakuru 77 C3
Namib Desert 11 D2, 86 A3
Namibe 68 B1
Nampula 81 D4
Nanyuki 77 C4
Nasser, Lake 11 F7, 53 J1
Natron, Lake 77 C3
Nchanga 81 B4
N'Djamena 11 D6, 68 B6
Ndola 81 B4
Nelspruit 87 E2
Ngaoundéré 59 G2
Nguru 59 G3
Niamey 11 C6, 59 E3
Niger, r. 11 B6, 59 F2
Nile, r. 11 F7, 53 J2, 73 C5

Nimba, Mount 58 C2
Nkongsamba 59 F1
Nossob, r. 87 B3
Nouadhibou 58 A5
Nouakchott 10 A6, 58 A4
Nubian Desert 11 F7, 73 C6
Nyala 72 A4
Nyeri 77 C3

Ogbomosho 59 E2
Okavango Delta 11 E3, 87 C4
Olifants, r. 87 E3
Omdurman 73 C6
Onitsha 59 F2
Oran 52 D3
Orange, r. 11 E2, 87 B2
Oshogbo 59 E2
Ouagadougou 11 B6, 59 D3
Ouahigouya 59 D3
Oudtshoorn 87 C1
Oujda 52 D3

Paarl 87 B1
Palma, i. 52 A2
Palmas, Cape 10 B5, 58 C1
Pangani, r. 77 C2
Parakou 59 E2
Pemba 81 E4
Pemba, i. 11 F4, 77 C2
Pietermaritzburg 87 E2
Pietersburg 87 D3
Pointe Noire 68 A3
Port Elizabeth 87 D1
Port Gentil 68 A3
Port Harcourt 59 F1
Porto Novo 11 C5, 59 E2
Port Said 53 J3
Port Sudan 73 D5
Potchefstroom 87 D2
Praia 58 I7
Pretoria 11 E2, 87 D2
Príncipe, i. 11 C5, 68 A4

Qattara Depression 11 E7, 53 I2
Queenstown 87 D1
Quelimane 81 D3
Que Que 81 B3

Rabat 11 B8, 52 C3
Ras Dashan, mt. 11 F6, 73 D4
Red Sea 11 F7, 53 J2, 73 E5
Rovuma, r. 81 D4
Rufiji, r. 77 C2

Rukwa, Lake 77 B2
Rungwe, Mount 11 F4, 77 B2
Ruvuma, r. 77 C1
Ruwenzori Range, mts. 77 B4

Safi 52 C3
Sahara 11 C7, 52 E1, 59 G5
Saharan Atlas, mts. 52 E3
Sahel 11 F4, 59 F3
Saint Louis 58 A4
Sal, i. 58 I7
Sanaga, r. 59 G1
Santo Antão, i. 58 I7
São Nicolau, i. 58 I7
São Tiago, i. 58 I7
São Tomé 11 C5, 68 A4
São Tomé, i. 11 C5, 68 A4
São Vincente, i. 58 I7
Sarh 68 C5
Save, r. 81 C2
Segou 59 C3
Sekondi Takoradi 59 D2
Senegal, r. 10 A6, 58 A4
Setif 52 E4
Sfax 53 F3
Shebelle, r. 11 G5, 73 E3
Shire, r. 81 C3
Sidi Ifni 52 C2
Sikasso 59 C3
Sinai 11 F7, 53 J2
Sirte, Gulf of 53 G3
Siwa 53 I2
Sokode 59 E2
Sokoto 59 F3
Sousse 53 F3
Stanley, Mount 11 E5, 68 D4
Sudd 11 E5, 73 C3
Suez 53 J3
Suez Canal 11 F8, 53 J3
Suez, Gulf of 53 J2
Swakopmund 86 A3

Table Mt. 87 B1
Tabora 77 B2
Tademait, Plateau of 52 E2
Tahat, Mount 11 C7, 52 E1
Tamale 59 D2
Tana, r. 77 D3
Tana, Lake 11 F6, 73 D4
Tanga 77 C2
Tanganyika, Lake 11 F4, 68 D3, 77 B2
Tangier 52 D3
Tanta 53 J3
Tekeze, r. 73 D4

Tenerife, i. 52 B2
Tete 81 C3
Thabana Ntlenyana, mt. 87 D2
Tibesti, mts. 11 D7, 68 B7
Timbuktu 59 D4
Toubkal, mt. 11 B8, 52 C3
Tripoli 11 D8, 53 G3
Tubruq 53 H3
Tunis 11 D8, 53 F4
Turkana, Lake 11 F4, 77 C4

Ubangi, r. 11 D5, 68 C4
Ubundu 68 D3
Uele, r. 68 D4
Ugab, r. 86 A3
Uitenhage 87 D1
Upington 87 C2

Vaal, r. 11 E2, 87 D2
Vereeniging 87 D2
Victoria, Lake 11 F4, 77 B3
Victoria Falls 81 B3
Voi 77 C3
Volta, r. 59 E2
Volta, Lake 11 B5, 59 D2

Wadi Halfa 73 C6
Wad Medani 73 C4
Wajir 77 C4
Walvis Bay 11 D2, 86 A3
Wami, r. 77 C2
Wau 72 B3
Welkom 87 D2
White Nile, r. 11 F6, 73 C4, 77 B4
Windhoek 11 E2, 86 B3
Worcester 87 B1

Xai-Xai 81 C1

Yamoussoukro 11 B5
Yaoundé 11 D5, 59 G1

Zambezi, r. 11 F3, 81 C3
Zanzibar 77 C2
Zanzibar, i. 11 F4, 77 C2
Zaria 59 F3
Ziguinchor 58 A3
Zinder 59 F3
Zomba 81 D3
Zumbo 81 C3

# Index

Page numbers in *italics* refer to illustrations or their captions.

Africa
central 12, *15*, 17, 24, 33;
East 10, 17, 24, 32, 36, 38, 39, 69, 76–77, 78–79, *90*;
eastern 10, 14, 15, 22;
Horn of 32, 54, 72;
North 12, *13*, 15, 16, 18–19, 30, *31*, 34, 36, 52–53;
northeast 12, 72–73;
South *14*, 26, 27, 30, *31*, *36*, *37*, 39, *39*, *44*, *81*, 84, *85*, 86, 88, 90;
southern 14, 15, *15*, 17, 31, 38, 69, 86–87, 88;
southeast central 80–81;
southwest 12;
West 12, 15, 16, 24, 32, 36, 37, 54, 58–59, 64, 84;
west central 12, 36, 39, 46, 68–69
African National Congress (ANC) 86
African Union (AU) 90, *91*
Afrikaans 39
Agades 37
AIDS 86
al-Azhar University *56*
Albert, Lake *28*
Alexander the Great 18, 19
Alexandria 18, 19, 32
Algeria 16, 31, *37*, *38*, *52*, 53, 54
Angola 30, *31*, *44*, 69, *69*
animals 12, *13*, 54, 60, *69*, 76, *78*, 82, 88;
sacrifices 34, *34*, 62, *63*, 75
apartheid 86
Arabic *38*, 40, 52, 68
Arab League 90, *91*
Arabs 16, 17, 20, 22, *22*, 24, 52, 56
arts and crafts *20*, *30*, 41, 42–43, 66–67
Asante 17, *47*, 64–65
Atlas Mountains *52*
Augustus 18, 19
*Australopithecus africanus* 15
Axum *16*, 17, 74, *74*

Bantu
languages 39, *39*, 69, 71, 76, 80, 86;
-speaking peoples *15*, *27*, 68, 86, 88;
states 17
Baulé *39*, *43*
bazaars *56*
Bedouin *54*

Belgian colonies and influence 21, 30, 68, 76
Beni Abbes *21*
Benin 17, *39*, *44*, 62, 66, *66*
Berber 16, 19, 20, 32, 52, 54;
language *38*, 52
Biafra 58
Blood River *26*
Boers, the 26, 27, *27*
Borno 17
Botswana 86, *86*, 88
Brazzaville 37
British colonies and influence 21, 24, 25, 26, 53, 56, 58, 65, 72, 76, 80, 86, 90
bronze *see* metals
Buganda 29, 31, 76
buildings 48, 82;
*see also* dwellings; houses
Burkina Faso 58, 60
Burundi 38, 76
Bushmen 38, *38*;
*see also* San

Cabora Bassa Dam *81*
Cairo 37, 41, 56–57
Cameroon *44*;
Mount *58*
Canary Islands 52
Cape of Good Hope 21, 22, 26, 39
Cape Town 21, 27, 37
Cape Verde 58
Carthage 16, 17, 18, 19, 32, 37
Central African Federation 80
Central African Republic 69
ceremonies and festivals 35, 42, 43, *45*, 60, *62*, 64–65, 75;
funerals 35, *44*, 64
Chad 14, *46*, 54, 68, 69, *69*;
Lake 10, 12, 17
Chaka Zulu 17
Christianity and christians 16, 18, 22, 30–31, 32, 34, 58, 68, 72, 74–75, 76
churches 27, 30, 52, 74, *74*, 75, *75*
cities 36, 37, *37*
city-states 17, *17*, 22
Cleopatra 18, 19
climate 10, 12–13, 17, 52
cloth 17, 70
clothing 60, 65, 70, *71*, *79*, *86*
Congo
river 28;
*see also* Democratic Republic of Congo;
Republic of Congo
copper *see* metals
Copper Belt, the 69, 80, 84, 85

Coptic *38*;
church 56, 75
Côte d'Ivoire 39, *43*
Cotonou Agreement 90, *91*
crops 17, 54, 60, 69, *69*, 76, 80, 82
Cyrenaica 19
Cyrene 19

da Gama, Vasco 20, 22
dance 44–45, *62*, 63, 71
Dar es Salaam 37
Darwin, Charles 14
debt relief 90
Democratic Republic of Congo *8*, 17, 20, 30, *30*, *31*, *42*, *44*, 68, 69, 70, *71*, 84, *84*, *85*
deserts 12, *13*, 36, *52*, 54, 58, 68;
*see also* Sahara; Kalahari
diamonds 20, 27, *69*, 84, *85*, 86
Dias, Bartholomeu 21, 22
Dinka *38*, *41*
Djibouti 72
Dogon *5*, *44*, 60
Dorobo 70
Dougga *18*
drawings
rock 19, 42
Durban *41*
Dutch colonies and influence 21, 25, 26, 30, 86;
East India Company 21, 26
dwellings *17*, 60, 70;
*see also* houses

Eastern Rift *10*
Economic Commission for Africa (ECA) 90, *91*
education 21, 40–41
Egypt 16, 17, 18, 19, *20*, 28, *28*, 30, 32, 36, *37*, *38*, *52*, 53, *53*, 56
elders 16, 41, 76
El Djem *18*
Elgon, Mt. *12*
Eritrea 72
Ethiopia 15, *16*, 17, 21, 22, 30, 32, 34, 37, 38, 72, 74–75, 90
Europeans 16, 20–21
explorers 21, 82

farmers and farming *13*, 26, 27, *27*, *46*, 60, 68, 70, 76, 86
fishing 60, 68, 79, *90*
food 22, *22*, 60, 76, 78, 88
Fort Jesus 22, *22*
fortune-telling 35, *42*, 63, *63*

fossils 14, *14*
French colonies and influence 21, *21*, 24, 25, 26, 30, 53, 56, 58, 68, 69, 72, 86, 90;
Foreign Legion *21*;
Equatorial Africa 69
Fulani (Fulbe) 68, 69

Gabon *37*, 68, 69, *69*
Gambia 58
game parks 78–79
Ganda 29, 76
German colonies and influence 21, 24, 30, 76
Ghana 17, 21, *31*, *34*, *47*, 58, 64, 65
gods, goddesses, and spirits 18, 34, 62, *62*, 63, *63*, 71
gold *see* metals
Gold Coast *see* Ghana
Great Rift Valley *10*, *11*, 76, *76*
Great Trek, the 26–27
Greeks 18–19, 52
Guinea
Gulf of *58*
Equatorial 69
Spanish *see* Guinea, Equatorial
Guinea-Bissau 58

Hannibal 19
herders 38, 54, 60, 68, 76, 82, 88
Herero *86*
Hoggar, the 54
*Hogon* 60
*Homo*
*erectus* 14, 15
*habilis* 14, 15
*sapiens* 15
Hottentots *see* Khoikhoi
houses 27, *39*, 46–47, 76, *79*
hunters and hunting 14, 71, 79
hunter-gatherers 12, *13*, 14, 15, 38, 68, 70, 86, 88–89
Husuni Kubwa 48
Hutu 76

Ibadan 37
Ibn Battuta 20
Ife 66, *66*
Igbo 16, 17
iron *see* metals
Iron Age 15
Islam *16*, 17, 30, *31*, 32–33, 34, 52, 58, 72, 76
Italian colonies and influence 21, 30, 72
ivory 17, *19*, 21, *22*, 24, *42*, 82

Judaism and the Jews 32, 72, 75
Johannesburg 27, *36*

Kababis *54*
Kabaka (king) *29*, 76
Kabyle *38*
Kalahari Desert 54, *86*, 88
Kampala 37
Kanem 17
Kanem-Bornu 17
Kano (city) *17*, 37, *40*, *43*
Kariba
Dam *78*, *81*;
Lake *78*
Kasulu *28*
Katanga 69
Kenya 10, *12*, 14, 15, 16, 30, 39, *39*, *54*, 70, 76, 90;
Mount 10, *76*
Khartoum *34*, *72*
Khoekhoe *38*, *38*, 86, 88
Khoisan 86
Kikuyu 16, 76
Kilimanjaro, Mt. *10*, 76
Kilwa 17, 22, 48
Kindiga 70
kingdoms 16–17, 76;
*see also* Buganda;
Lesotho
Kinshasa 37
Kiswahili *see* Swahili
Kongo 17, 69
Kush 16

Lagos 37
Lalibela 75, *75*
languages 21, 38–39, 41, 52, 58, 68, 69, *69*, 74, 76;
*see also* Afrikaans; Arabic;
Bantu; Berber; Coptic;
Swahili
Lesotho 17, *26*, 85, 86, *86*
Liberia 21, 58
Libya 53
Limpopo river *81*
Livingstone, David *28*, 80
Loango 69
Luba *42*

Maasai 70, *78*, 79, *79*
Madagascar *10*, 39, *43*
Malawi *10*, 80, *81*;
Lake 12
Mali *8*, 17, 32, 35, *44*, 58
Malindi 22
Mau-Mau 76
Mauretania 16, 19
Mauritania 19, 32, 90
Mbuti 38, 70
Memphis 56

metals 17, *22*, 24, 42, 67, *69*, 82;
  bronze and brass 66;
  copper 20, 84;
  gold 17, 20, 21, *22*, 24, 27, 28, *36*, 65, 82, 86;
  iron 15, *15*, *69*, 84
minerals 28, 36, *69*, 80, 84–85;
  *see also* diamonds; metals
missionaries 21, 22, 28, *29*, 30–31, 41, *86*;
  Society of Missionaries of Africa (White Fathers) 30;
  Societies 31, *86*
Mogadishu 17, 22
Mombasa 22, 31
Monomutapa 82
Morocco 16, *37*, 53, *54*, 84
Moshoeshoe 17
Mosque
  Faron *34*;
  Friday *35*
mosques *8*, 21, 33, *33*, 56, *56*;
  *see also* Mosque
mountains 12, 36
Mozambique *10*, 22, 30, 31, *39*, 80
music 25, 44–45, *65*, 75
Muslims 16, *16*, 17, 22, 37, *40*, 41, 54, 56, 68, *69*, 72, 80;
  *see also* Islam

Nairobi *30*
Namibia 36, *37*, 84, 86, *86*, 88, 90
Natal *26*
Ndongo 69
Ngindo *42*
Ngola 17

Niger 32, *37*;
  river 28, *28*, 36, *58*, 60
Nigeria 16, 17, *17*, 31, *31*, *37*, *40*, *43*, *44*, *46*, *58*, 62, 66
Nile 16, 28, *28*, *34*, 72
nomadic
  life 54–55;
  people 52, 60, 68, *69*, 72, 76
Nuba *46*
Nubia 32
Nubians *47*
Numidia 16, 19
Nupe *46*
Nyasaland *see* Malawi

Olduvai Gorge 14, *14*
Operation Noah *78*
Orange Free State 27
Orange River 27
Organization of African Unity (OAU) 72, 90

paintings, cave *14*, 42
Pangea 10
peoples 38–39;
  *see also* Baulé; Bedouin; Berbers; Dinka; Dogon; Dorobo; Fulani; Ganda; Herero; Hutu; Igbo; Kababis; Kabyle; Khoikhoi; Khoisan; Kikuyu; Kindiga; Luba; Maasai; Mau-Mau; Mbuti; Ngindo; Nuba; Nubians; Nupe; San; Shilluk; Shona; Somali; Sotho; Tuareg; Tutsi; Xhosa; Yoruba; Zulu
Phoenicians 16, 17, 18, 19, 52

plateaux 10, *11*, 12, 72
poaching *78*
population 17, 36–37
Portuguese colonies and influence 17, 20, 21, 22, 30, *30*, *31*, 58, 68, 69
pottery *15*, 22
Ptolemy 18, 19
Ptolemy, Claudius 20
pygmies 68, 69, 70–71

Qattara Depression, the *52*

rainfall 12, 13
rainforest 12
Rand, the 84, 86
religions 34–35, 58, 62–63, 68, 72, 74, 80, *86*;
  *see also* Christianity; Islam; Judaism
Republic of Congo 17, 31, *44*, 69, *69*
Rhodesia
  Northern *see* Zambia;
  Southern *see* Zimbabwe
rift 10, *10*
Romans 18–19, 52
Rwanda 76

Sahara 12, *14*, 17, 19, 32, 36
*Sahelanthropus tchadensis* 14
Sahel Desert 54
San *14*, 38, *38*, 70, 86, 88, *88*
schools *see* education
Sarwa *46*
seasons 12, *13*
Senegal *43*, 58, 90
settlers 21, 26, 76
Shango *34*
shantytowns 27, 36, 47
Shilluk *72*

Shona 82, 83
Sierra Leone 30, 31, *45*, 58
slaves *19*, 21, *22*, 62;
  trade 17, 24–25, 28, 66
Sofala 22, *22*
Sokoto 37
Somali 32, *54*
Somalia 22, *31*, 38, 54, *54*, 72, *72*, 90
Songhay 17
Sotho 27, *27*
Spanish colonies and influence 21, 53, 68
Stanley, Henry Morton 28, *29*
Stone Age 15;
  Early *14*;
  Middle *14*
Sudan 28, 30, *31*, 32, 34, 36, 38, *38*, *39*, 41, *54*, 72, *72*, 90
Suez Canal 53, 56
Swahili 39, 41
Swaziland *26*, 86

Tanganyika 76
Tanzania *12*, 14, 15, 33, 39, *39*, 42, 48, 70, 76, 84
temperature 12–13
tents 54, *54*
Timbuktu *33*
Togo 62
tools *14*, 15
traders 16, 17, 21, 22;
  slave 24
trades 20
trading 16, 19, *19*, *20*, 22, 25, *25*, 32
Transvaal 27
Tuareg 54
Tunisia 53
Tunis 37

Turkana, Lake *14*
Tutsi 38, 76

Uganda 15, *29*, 39, *44*, 72, 76
Ujiji 28
United States, the 16, 24, 58

vegetation 12–13
Victoria Falls *80*
Victoria, Lake 12, *28*, *29*, 36
villages 36, 46–47, *53*, 60, 69
Volta River *58*;
  Upper 58

war 53, 58, 76, 80;
  Algerian 53;
  Anglo–Boer 27, 86;
  civil 58, 69, 72, 76, 80;
  Punic 19;
  Six-day 53;
  Yom Kippur 53
Western Sahara 52
witchdoctors 35

Xhosa 27, *27*, 36, 41

Yoruba 17, *30*, 42, *45*, 62–63

Zaïre *see* Democratic Republic of Congo
Zambezi river *80*, *81*
Zambia *44*, 80, *80*, 84, *84*, 85
Zanzibar 76, *76*, 90
Zimbabwe *31*, 80, *80*, *81*, 82–83;
  Great 17, 82–83
Zulu *26*, 27, *27*